COMING TOGETHER

. . . by BROCK TULLY

A 10,000 MILE BICYCLE JOURNEY

First Printing - July 1972

Cover Photography by Chris Dadson

From Cosmopolitan World Map
© 1989 by Rand McNally & Co., R.L. 89-S224

ISBN 0-969-3583-4-2

Brock Tully
Apt. #706 - 2222 Bellevue Ave.,
West Vancouver, B.C.,
Canada, V7V-1C7
(604)922-8440

- thankyou to Rand McNally and Co.
  for permission to use a portion of
  one of their maps.

... since my bicycle trip, I've written three Reflection books of inspirational thoughts ...

     1. "Reflections - for someone special"
     2. "Reflections - for living life fully"
     3. "Reflections - for touching hearts"

... I've included many of these thoughts throughout this revised edition of "Coming Together" to show how much I've changed in so many aspects of my life. I hope I continue to change and 'grow' on my exciting journey to be closer to my heart.

... I have also now written "With Hope We Can All Find Ogo Pogo" - a story about staying in touch with our hearts and the child, i believe, is within us all.

ACKNOWLEDGEMENTS

Of the entire book, this is the most difficult part to write. The names of people who have helped me keep going by giving me faith in people, not only on my trip, but all through my life, would be an endless list. To them I'd like to give a great big Thank-You!

There are a few, however, to whom I would like to give special thanks...

    ... since I decided to reprint "Coming Together", I also wanted to re-edit it as well. A special friend, Rosie, suggested Louise Amm. Now that I am led by my intuition, I knew the moment I met her warm heart, that she was the right person for this project.

    ... secondly, I would like to acknowledge the time and effort of Chris Dadson, who did the photography. It is really a pleasure working with someone who is really "into" something and not just doing it because it was a job.

    ... I would like to thank my wonderful and special family who, although many times, have had trouble understanding me, have accepted and stood beside me all the same.

    ... Finally, I would like to sincerely thank all my closest friends for believing in me, and for giving me the extra strength to take the risk to undertake this wonderful journey.

With Love Always,

Brock

ABOUT THE AUTHOR

When Brock set out on his 10-speed bike from Vancouver, I doubt if anyone - outside a few close friends
who fully understand the intensity of spirit by which he
ensures the adequate discharge of any undertaking - believed that he would make it to the West Indies. And,
certainly, no one could have predicted that he would
eventually want to continue, far past his intended point
of departure for the islands.

In retrospect, though, while it was highly unlikely
that anyone could have predicted that Brock would become
so strongly motivated to ride on, it is completely understandable. But to appreciate this one must first gain some
insight into the character that is Brock Tully.

It can be said of Brock, more than any other person
I know, that he has empathy. This incredible "feeling" for
people complements a complete honesty and great wit.
Consequently, Brock has a wonderful way with people. When
talking with Brock one quickly gets the feeling that here
is a person whose expressed concern and interest are real-
that one's own problems, so long as they are not trivial,
are his problems.

Brock has developed what might be called a very
sensible and undistorted "people perspective." He could
not manage without this. In helping others in the pursuit
of happiness, as he must, and in helping himself, "people
perspective" is a requisite.

Perhaps now we can understand that Brock's adven-
ture became a people trip. His decision to continue riding
derived from a growing obsession with meeting and trying
to understand people in their unique natural environ-
ments, and, above all, with wanting intensely to do
something constructive about all the sad things to which
he had inevitably been exposed. This book is, quite
naturally then, a partial elaboration of "people
perspective."

Willie Cheyne

September, 1989 - PRE-INTRODUCTION

Almost to the day, it's been 19 years since I began my six-month 10,000 mile bicycle journey and 18 years since I finished writing this book about it.

Because it was such a major turning point in my life, I decided to have *"COMING TOGETHER"* reprinted.

It was very tough, in many respects, to ride a bicycle through the United States in 1970 - there was the Vietnam War, the black-white racial riots, and the hippie/red-neck conflict. These were all life-threatening to me during the trip, but the toughest part was the decision to do the trip - to take the risk to follow my heart and go after my dreams - *TO LIVE LIFE!*

I am now able to see that there may be the risk of dying doing something I'd love to do, but there is certain death in being afraid and not doing it.

Before the bicycle trip, I was afraid to write. Now that I am seeing that success isn't accomplishments, but *LOVING THE JOURNEY*, I am more able to write from my heart and I am loving it!

I have now written three *"REFLECTIONS"* books and a children's book for grownups. The first *"REFLECTIONS"* was dedicated to Gandhi, Martin Luther King, and Winnie-the-Pooh.

It's movies like "The Dead Poet's Society" that constantly remind me of the first thought I ever wrote, and which I need to constantly remind myself of ...

"i'd rather be seen
for who i am
and be alone ...

than to be accepted
for somebody i'm not
and be lonely."

I do hope you enjoy my journey, through this book,
but I <u>especially</u> hope it touches you in a way you,
too, will follow your heart, so that your dreams
will no longer be your dreams, but your reality...

" ... i'll never find out
what i can do ...

unless i do all i can
to find out."

Brock Tully

INTRODUCTION – 1971

I will never forget September 8, 1970. It was the first day of the most fantastic experience of my life, and I had no idea then that six months later I would have travelled through half the states of the United States and all of Mexico on my ten-speed bicycle.

I never really decided to leave on my trip until about two weeks before my actual departure date. I knew I wanted to take a year out from university as, after four years of physical education and psychology, I was still not sure of my plans following graduation. I still had another year to go to get my degree in the Education Faculty, but I felt it would be a wasted year to go back to university when I still wasn't sure of what I wanted to do. Therefore, I decided to head for the West Indies. The attraction there was the beautiful beaches with clear, unpolluted water, and, of course, the sun which, by itself, makes me feel very happy. It slows down and relaxes me and gives me a healthy feeling.

But having arrived in Miami, I had a sudden change in plans and heart. The eye-opening and rewarding experience of 3,000 miles of bicycling con- vinced me to continue riding on through the southern States and eventually to doing a figure eight covering all of Mexico and then returning to the States in Arizona. Once back in the States, I headed further west to Los Angeles from where I flew to Hawaii to visit my vacationing parents. After a two-week rest I returned to Los Angeles from where I headed east again with the hope of visiting the States I had thus far not visited. But in Texas my trip was terminated as I had developed a pilanidal cyst on my posterior and I had to return home by airplane.

ARLINGTON

Anthony and I woke up early to the sound of
the alarm. It was about the worst sound I've heard,
so I passed it off as not happening, and just rolled
over for some more sleep. Such was not the case
with Anthony, however, as he was anxious to hit the
road. This, I think, was my first realization that
the whole idea of a trip was serious and not just
some kind of far-fetched dream which, at this point,
I was hoping would be the case.

Anthony was in my physical education class at
the school where I was student-teaching. He had
failed his physical education course, mainly, I
think, because he disagreed with the way it was being taught. (I tend to agree with him especially
in view of the fact that he was undertaking a
physical challenge that very few people would under-
take and yet he failed physical education. I think
there is something drastically wrong somewhere.)
Anthony's strength and determination made my turning
back an impossibility.

Then I heard what should definitely have swayed
our decision towards cancelling the whole silly trip.
It was a little pitter-patter noise of rain on the
roof which Anthony soon confirmed when he looked out
the window at the grey, gloomy sky. I smiled when I
heard this, hoping it was a good enough excuse for
my staying in the security of Vancouver for the winter. My face soon dropped, however, as I detected
an even more determined look on Anthony's face.
Although I realized now that the trip was a serious
thing, I never lost faith until we had actually left
the outskirts of Vancouver that something was going
to prevent us from going.

Although we were up by about 6:00, our early
rise didn't prevent us from hitting the rush hour
traffic, as we spent our last sure and secure moments in slow preparation for what lay ahead. We
finally got away and it didn't take long before we

were able to ignore the slight drizzle of rain. Actually the traffic didn't bother us, it even encouraged us, as we were able to recognize a few faces that provided us with a little inspiration.

From our homes in West Vancouver, we headed across the Lion's Gate Bridge into downtown Vancouver, out to Kingsway, and into New Westminster, then through Surrey and a few small country towns, and finally across the border into the United States. At the border I bought a postcard which I planned on sending to friends in a few weeks. I was going to say that this was how far I'd gotten after a few weeks' riding. I thought this little touch would be good for a few chuckles.

It was a very enjoyable day as far as riding was concerned as the terrain was fairly flat, but we knew that tomorrow was going to be a different story as the mountains were staring us in the face. The beautiful scenery and flat land was made considerably less enjoyable by the pain that I was going through. It was a terifically sharp pain through one of my knees every time I put pressure on the pedal, and to avoid pressure on the pedal would have meant no mileage on the bicycle. Therefore, to keep pace with Anthony I had to put up with the agony.

We had a very frightening experience today as well, which I'm sure was a forewarning of the dangers to come. It made daydreaming impossible, and concentration a necessity which can be just as tiring as the physical fatigue from pedalling. We were narrowly missed by a huge truck. When I say narrowly, I mean by no more than an inch.

A more pleasant feature of the day's ride was the blackberry bushes along the roadside. During one of our few short stops, we ate our fill of these blackberries and we almost had to assist each other back onto our bicycles - we had stuffed ourselves so much.

Where to stay became a very big and scary
thought to us now as the sun had set and we were
just entering the small town of Arlington in Washington State. Our search for a campground met with
failure so we headed out into the blackness of the
night to find some bushes that would hide our pup-
tent somewhere along the main highway. Just outside
of Arlington was our biggest climb of the day which
was made more difficult by our fatigue. After eleven
hours and 135 miles we finally found a suitable spot
and tne little pup-tent was set up and occupied in
the shortest time possible. Sleep, however, didn't
come easily as my system was still going about a
hundred miles an hour. I just lay there awake for
quite awhile thinking about the dreadful day that lay
ahead of us.

WENATCHEE

When we started out this morning I had no idea
that we would be spending the evening in Wenatchee.
I was really looking forward to getting to Wenatchee as a friend of mine, Nancy Allen, whom I have
not seen for many years, lives there. Judging the
distance from Arlington to Wenatchee, we should have
gotten there by tomorrow night at the earliest. Fortunately, or unfortunately, depending on how I look
at it, we were able to get a lift in a pick-up truck
for part of the way there. I say fortunately because
it was the tough part of the way. He took us about
forty miles on one side of the mountains, and it
wouldn't take much to guess which side. I said unfortunately because at the present moment I am having
guilt feelings from having cheated. We hadn't asked
for the ride and the offer was just too tempting to
pass up. Besides, I honestly doubt that I could have
made it as there was no improvement in my knee and I
was actually becoming very worried that I was going
to have to return home. I think the only thing that
was keeping me going was my pride.

When we arrived the first thing I did was to
phone Nancy. She was staying with a group of people

in an orchard on the outskirts of Wenatchee who were there for the purpose of an "archaelogical dig". It was a commune-type arrangement and the people said we were welcome to stay there for the evening. Nancy and I reminisced briefly about old times and everyone retired early as all of us had a long day ahead. They, too, enjoyed the early part of the morning when the sun rose over the distant mountains.

ODESSA

We were awakened early by the scurrying of many feet as the people all prepared to head out to the "dig". We agreed to meet them when we had gotten all our gear together. I really don't know how they could stand all the dust that engulfed them as they chiselled at the dry dirt, looking with meticulous care for fragile artifacts. There was no way that I could have the patience that these people had, but I guess it requires patience only if you're not truly involved and interested in what you're doing. There-fore, I guess there is no such thing as patience if you're enjoying something.

After we left Nancy and the others, Anthony and I headed out into the dry, open country of the interi-or of Washington State which became progressively hot-ter as the sun moved westward. In one long stretch, Anthony and I were completely without water and we be-came very worried to say the least as a town wasn't on the map for many, many miles. Fortunately, we found a lonely little farmhouse where we got a welcome refill for the water jug.

After coasting down a long, straight downhill stretch that led into Odessa, we were greeted by two young college students who were just preparing to go to school in Spokane for the winter session. One of them, Steve, invited us to stay at his parents' farm which was about eight miles out of town. We threw our bicycles in the back of his truck and proceeded to travel the gravel road that led to his house. We had dinner, then the three of us went out to a grass area where Steve pitched a big tent for us, which seemed like a mansion in comparison to my little two-man pup-tent. The pup-tent I have, incidentally, is only five feet long, not the six feet as was stated on the box, so it was always going to be a big decision whether to have our feet or our heads hanging out the door. Steve's farm went for many miles in all directions and situated in the centre was a fairly large lake where they fished and waterskiied. Along one side of the lake were some towering cliffs from which the braver people (of which I certainly wasn't one) did flying leaps. But the best part of the whole farm without a doubt was Steve. He was one of the warmest, kindest, and most giving persons I have ever met. Meeting a person like him has made all my ailments really minor things and he has inspired me to continue my trip in a more optimistic fashion.

MISSOULA

After breakfast Anthony and I rode as far as Coeur d'Alene before meeting our newest obstacle. A cold spell had come down from the north and the below-freezing weather was extremely unusual for this time of year. The wind was no help for our misery and finally our hands and faces became just too cold for riding. The weather report was for continuing cold so we thought that the best thing for us to do was just to hitch-hike on to where the weather might be more agreeable.

After waiting for what seemed like days, but was probably only about half an hour, a fellow in a car pulled over and gave us and our bicycles a ride into Missoula. Our conversation was very limited as he continuously guzzled beer, but between mouthfuls we did learn that he was heading for college in Missoula. He drove us to a campsite on the outskirts of town which was fairly deserted.

As the darkness of the night surrounded us it became increasingly colder and it was almost unbearable as we had brought no clothes for this type of

weather. It was now down to about 20 degrees but felt
colder. I set up the tent as fast as I could, which
was a very difficult and slow task as my hands were
so frozen by now that clutching a rock to bang in the
spikes was almost an impossibility. While I was fum-
bling through this chore, Anthony was trying to bring
back his boyscout skills as he attempted to build a
fire. Finally both jobs were completed but our feelings of satisfaction for a job well done soon disappeared when we realized that the fire was built on the
wrong side of the tent. The wind was blowing the
sparks right toward the tent and I'm sure that at this
point we could have sat down and cried. We found it
much easier to put out the fire than to get it started
and it wasn't long before we were tucked away in the
freezing little tent. We lay there shaking and we
both knew we had a long, cold, sleepless night ahead
of us.

BOZEMAN

As I crawled out of the tent in the morning I was
almost blinded by the brightness of our white sur-
roundings. It had snowed during the night and my
first thought was to just climb back into my sleeping
bag. But I realized that things would only get worse
and that we had better get out of these mountains as
fast as possible. Our bags were a bit lighter as some
little animal had stolen the peanut butter sandwiches
I had made for breakfast.

We rode our bicycles as far as we could before
the weather became the victor. In Butte we stood beside the road hitch-hiking for at least two hours. A
lady and her husband stood in a nearby motel window
watching us in complete bewilderment as we yelled, ran
around in circles, and did other little crazy antics
to keep from getting frostbite.

We were continually getting word from passers-by
that the mountain road had pretty well closed down
except to the more daring souls as there had been quite
a bit of snow during the day. Finally a brave person

who decided he was going to chance it, stopped and gave us a lift. We appreciated his thoughtfulness but I'm sure he must have also thought it would be nice to have an extra bit of muscle along in case he should get stuck. Little did he know that our strength at this point was at a low ebb, but we were very sure to keep this little fact to ourselves.

Well, we got as far as Bozeman as this was the end of the fellow's trip, but, as we were still well up in the mountains, we decided to continue our hitch-hiking. It was still light out so we headed for the outskirts of town and stuck out our thumbs just across from a Dairy Queen. They didn't seem to mind too much one of us warming up in there while the other desperately, but without luck, attempted to get us a ride. We then happily found some girls who lived together in a house who invited us to stay the evening and I'm sure they've never heard such a quick response. We certainly had no intention of playing hard to get.

BILLINGS

We rolled out of bed sometime before noon, I think, then headed directly to the good old Dairy Queen again where we stuck out our thumbs. It wasn't long before the freezing weather had our arms frozen in this po-sition and they stayed that way for a long time as a ride was very hard to come by. I must admit that to-day Anthony and I went completely nuts. Normally, two sensible and mature people, we were anything but that today - singing, dancing, giggling, poking, just to keep ourselves from freezing to death.

We finally got a ride and we were enlightened as to why people were so hesitant to give rides in these parts. Apparently, not too long ago, a fellow had given a ride to two young people who were stoned on LSD. They killed the driver and ate his body. Later the two people were found in California with the fingers in their pockets. The fellow who picked us up said that the two must have kept the fingers for dessert. I told him he was safe as we had just eaten and his driving became noticeably more relaxed.

By the time we got to Billings it was nearing nightfall and after looking briefly around town our search for a warm place to stay was unsuccessful and we found ourselves in a train depot trying to think about our immediate plans. Hope of finding a place to stay had almost gone when we decided that we would inquire about any trains that might be leaving in an easterly direction. The conversation quickly ended, however, when we learned of the expense. The lady at the desk was very understanding of our situation and suggested that we should hop freight cars. When our eyes lit up she knew that she had aroused our adventuresome natures and so she phoned down to the freight office to find out when the next train came in. She also found out where it was headed and what track number it was on. It was simply unbelievable as it was just like having reservations. By the time we arrived at the tracks in the pitch black of the night we had become very scared at the thought but, nevertheless, decided that we had no alternative at this point but to carry things through.

The train finally arrived and we threw our bicycles and ourselves on a flat deck as there were no empty box cars. It was well below freezing and even our sleeping bags did very little to keep us warm as the cold breeze ran right through us. I got no sleep the whole night and Anthony and I just lay there all night exchanging a few miserable words whenever we were able to get up enough energy.

GLENDIVE

The night was actually spent in moving by our new mobile home from Billings to Glendive, Montana. It was pitch black so we had no worries of being caught by the local police, but as the sun started to come up it became clear to us that our sleeping bags were clearly visible to anyone who might be looking in our direction.

As the train came to a stop in Glendive we heard footsteps approaching from the rear. I was already to stick my hands out of my sleeping bag so that they could slip handcuffs on, but before I did, I heard a "pssst, pssst". Anthony and I peeked out of our bags to see two smiling hobos who informed us that there were a few empty box cars near the rear of the train. We gathered our things together and scrambled to the back of the train to our new home.

JAMESTOWN

I ran over to a nearby grocery store where I bought some milk, bread, and peanut butter. We had the most exciting little picnic before our departure.

Another freight train had come in on the tracks next to us and our two hobo friends decided to move their belongings onto it. We asked them why they changed trains and they replied that they just had a feeling it would leave first. We, however, decided to take our chances and stay. Naturally they had made the right choice and I suppose we will learn with experience. We waved to them sadly as they disappeared off in the distance. Finally our home began it's move and we sang and whistled as the countryside whipped by.

A very exciting moment for us was to cross the Missouri River just before entering Bismarck, the capitol of North Dakota. The land here is open and deserted and even small towns are scarce. Thank goodness we had the excuse of the cold weather to hop freight cars as otherwise it would have been very lonely and slow travelling through these parts.

We found out that during the night our box car had been switched onto another train bound for a different destination. It was going to Aberdeen, South Dakota, which was directly south of Jamestown. At first we were very upset, but quickly accepted the unexpected change in plans and it wasn't long before we just sat back and enjoyed the trip as though it were a holiday.

I had always pictured North and South Dakota as a big, barren mass of land, and thus a very boring part of the trip. On the contrary, it was a very worth-while and enjoyable part as the miles and miles of grassland and open country gave me a happy feeling of freedom and peacefulness.

To keep ourselves warm and also because we both had gone a little bonkers, we would occasionally have bicycle races from one end of the car to the other. We also wanted to be able to say that we rode our bi-cycles from North Dakota to South Dakota.

When we arrived in Aberdeen it had already gotten dark so we headed for the freight station that pointed in an easterly direction. We were both very tired and by now were fairly used to sleeping in freight cars. I doubt that I could get a good night's sleep on a soft bed that didn't jiggle and where there was a complete silence. At the station we found that there were no empty cars and that there were no trains going through tonight. In desperation we headed towards the centre of town where we came across a Mr. Mike's which was having a "two beers for one" night. This was a very appealing deal to me as I've really mis-sed relaxing over a nice cold beer. I became much more than relaxed, as did Anthony, and I'm sure we were in a state bordering on being drunk! We met some very aimiable people who offered us a nice warm place to stay. They jumped into their car and we pedalled along in a stupor after them. We listened to a few records before passing out.

MILBANK

The next thing I knew it was morning. Anyway, I was told it was around 8:30 and in no time I had hopped back into my cut-offs, singlet, sweater, and stinky running shoes, and was pedalling east.

Before leaving from our new "dream city" of Millbank, we stopped at Kentucky Fried Chicken for breakfast. We gorged ourselves and then headed out again against the elements.

Towns in this part of the country are far apart, but the wind made the distance between them much greater. We had to make one long climb today as well which cut down even more on our mileage, and just before we reached the summit of the mountain, we had more bad luck when we had an unwelcome shower that was obviously not going to let up. The rest of the way was downhill and would have brought a gleam to our eyes, but in the pouring rain, when brakes are unworkable, the danger makes it impossible to relax for a second and enjoy what would normally be a pleasure.

Just before entering Milbank, I swerved off the road accidentally onto a soft gravel shoulder and Anthony looked around just in time to see me spilling to the ground. By this time I was very tired and concentration was difficult.

Our first visit in Milbank was to one of the local laundromats to get all our gear and clothes dry. It was also a good shelter from the rain that continued falling. At the laundromat we got talking to a girl who invited us to stay at her place. She went to check with her roommate and soon returned with good news for us - that her "roomie" had agreed with her invitation. The only place to sleep was on the floor but we assured them that by now the floor was more condusive for us to sleep on than beds.

MINNEAPOLIS

It was 150 miles to Minneapolis. We rode our bicycles about a third of the way there, then hitchhiked the last part.

I suggested that we go to the Beta fraternity house where I was sure we would be able to get a room for the evening. The people we met there were very hospitable and even invited us to stay an extra evening as there was a party at the fraternity house. It really didn't take much to twist our arms as we

were already overdue for a little excitement and
socializing.

> " ... *as i learn*
> *to listen to my heart,*
> *i'm learning more & more*
>
> *that i need to unlearn*
> *the fears*
> *i learned before.*"

WINONA

I was filled with an entirely different feeling
as I headed out from Minneapolis this morning.
Anthony and I had split up and this was the first day
that I've faced alone. I will always remember the
good times Anthony and I had together and the beauties
of nature that we shared.

As soon as I lost sight of the mighty Mississippi
things became more unpleasant and I was almost ready
to turn around and go back and find Anthony. It is
really difficult to face miserable situations. Shared
misery never seems to be nearly as bad. Anyway, I
kept pushing on right into the face of one of the
strongest headwinds and I became progressively more
frustrated as I continued.

I only stayed in Rochester long enough to learn
that there was a small town called Winona some thirty
miles east of my present location that was highly popu-
lated with girls who attended three different all-
girl colleges.

The wind wasn't nearly as much trouble to me,
which was a great relief. With the biggest gasp of
relief I pedalled my way into Winona and prepared for
the mad rush of girls at the sight of a male in the
vicinity. Unfortunately such was not the case, but I
did manage to meet a group of people in a Kentucky
Fried Chicken place who offered to get me a shower and

a floor to spend the night on.

OSHKOSH

It wasn't long before I reached the Mississippi River this morning. I met many warm and friendly people in my short stay in La Crosse, so I left there with a beautiful feeling.

Part way to Oshkosh I had another flat tire and although it may seem a simple task to have it fixed, I have never attempted it and have always considered it an inconvenience that I would prefer to avoid. An offer from a girl in a car for a lift to a service station in Oshkosh certainly was a factor for putting off to another time having my first try at changing a flat tire.

> " ... *a big mistake, for me,*
> *is being afraid*
> *of making mistakes ...*
>
> *when i make this mistake,*
> *i make an even*
> *bigger mistake*
> *of being critical & unforgiving*
> *of those*
> *who make mistakes,*
>
> *and i don't see ...*
>
> *... the beautiful thing*
> *about making a mistake*
> *is that it is no longer*
> *a mistake*
> *if we learn from it.*"

KENOSHA

I set out early this morning in the hope that I could get to Chicago, some 150 miles, in the span of one day.

When I arrived in Kenosha about two-thirds of the

way to Chicago, a van pulled up beside me as I raced along. I carried on a conversation with a group of people who were hanging out of it wherever they found possible. They invited me to stop and join them at a park on the lake, and after another glance at the black sky, I quickly accepted their invitation as I felt a slight delay would be a very wise move. I was offered a place to lay my bed for the evening, as well as an invitation to a party in the park, so I put off Chicago until tomorrow.

One fellow that I met was very anxious to continue the trip with me to Washington, D.C., then down the east coast to Miami. He was all ready to sell his stereo equipment so that he could buy a bicycle. Although I sometimes think it would be great to have a companion, as times are often very lonely and miserable, I had to do all I could to persuade him to change his mind.

CHICAGO

By the time I had fought my way into Chicago it was already draped in the darkness of early evening. When I did look up, all I saw were thousands of Black people hanging out of windows, in large and many groups along the roadside, and packed into playgrounds, and they all seemed to have put down what they were doing as they looked in disbelief at this white creature who dared to pedal through their midst. Actually they did not all put down what they were doing. In fact, some of them even picked up rocks to hurl at the strange passerby and those who weren't as quick just shouted a few derogatory remarks in my direction. Once I was even asked to stop, and being the naive person that I am, I obliged, but I am sure that my stopping shocked them so much that by the time they had gotten over the surprise of someone being crazy enough to stop, I was able to sense their intentions and you've never, I am sure, seen anyone pedal so fast in your life.

When I arrived at the University of Chicago I headed directly for the security of the Beta Fraternity

House, which I found to have been dissolved as an organization only a few years ago. The house, however, had been taken over by a religious group from campus. Before I could leave, some of the more curious people at the door, having seen my bicycle and packs, inquired as to what exactly I was doing, and after learning that I was in the process of travelling around the States, they invited me in for dinner, washed and ironed my clothes, and gave me a place to rest for the night.

The campus was situated right in the middle of the Black section and it wasn't infrequent, I was told, that the college was faced with racial conflicts. Before heading off to bed I went to the college drugstore for a bedtime chocolate bar, but I high-tailed it home without getting this treat after I heard a few gun shots only a short distance away.

CHICAGO to PENNSBORO

The next week was filled with long days of riding and fairly uneventful but restful evenings. After Chicago I made my way in a southerly direction to Terre Haute, Indiana, then changed in a more easterly direction to Bloomington, a small but very comfortable town. I also spent a night in Cincinnati, and I was more than happy to leave there early the next morning. It wasn't that I disliked Cincinnati as a city, it was just that I'm finding coming into any large city for one night to be a very lonely thing. I was much happier to spend the following evening in Chillicothe, Ohio, and was feeling much more relaxed after a beautiful day of riding through the lush and green rolling and winding hills.

I stopped at a gas station just on the outskirts of Pennsboro and asked if they knew of any places where a person might spend the night at a reasonable price. The weather still doesn't make camping out a very attractive thought so I was thinking more in terms of a YMCA, cheap hotel, or the like.

He suggested a nearby rooming house, but also

added that he thought the rooms might only be available to construction workers. I decided it was worth a try anyway and I was in luck, but worried that my neighbours in adjoining rooms might be rowdy construction workers.

After grabbing a quick bite to eat I returned to my room for a good long night's sleep. Upon entering my room I noticed four guys who had already started a party just across the hall. I've seen mean and ugly drunks before and as I shut the door behind me I shook inside in fear that this might be the case tonight. I hadn't been lying there trembling for very long before I heard footsteps coming in the direction of my room and a knocking on my door.

I finally beckoned my visitors to enter and I was given a cordial invitation to join them which I hesitantly accepted, but I was still very wary of their intentions. We became very close friends in the shortest of time and they even insisted that I stay at least a week and that they could even get me a job on their crew. They soon realized, however, that as much as I wanted to stay I really had to keep on the move and Hook gave me a knife as a going away present to protect me from the snakes in the south.

Hook can make anything funny, but although he had a very humourous nature, he also is a very preceptive and compassionate person.

I went to bed much later than I had ever expected and I was very much prepared to wake up with a terrible hangover.

PENNSBORO (second night)

Hook, Wino, and the others had been at work on a new highway just adjacent to town only a few hours before I had managed to crawl out of bed. Before heading on to Washington, D.C., I had planned on stopping by where they worked to thank them for all that they had done for me and to bid them farewell. They suggested that I ride along the new highway that they were working on, which wasn't yet open to traffic, rather than the old bumpy road that they assured me was also winding and dangerous.

They either forgot to tell me about the barbed wire blockades where the old highway crossed the new one, or else they thought I was smart enough to go around them. If it was the latter, they made a drastic mistake in the judgment of my intelligence. Instead of going around them, I tried to go through them, although I must admit I had no idea the blockades were there until the last moment when it was already too late.

I slowly managed to get back onto my feet, holding my bleeding arms, and uttering a few nasty words in the process, completely oblivious to anyone's presence. However, I soon caught sight of a car out of the corner of my eye and I was stunned to see that it was occupied by nuns who all had their noses pressed up against the windows with expressions which showed that they were obviously shocked by my abusive language. My only apology was a meek, "oops!", followed by a shy "sorry!". They soon disappeared when they saw that help had quickly arrived.

I was taken to the hospital in an ambulance, which was absolutely unnecessary and an expense I would rather have done without.

After I was sufficiently nursed and bandaged I returned to my room in Pennsboro and to the surprised looks of my friends. Hook said that all day he had had a feeling that I would be back, but he never for a moment thought that I would be in this condition. I, too, wished it hadn't been this way.

We had a few more drinks together, saw a high-school football game, had a few more drinks, then I went to bed again hoping to head towards Washington in the morning.

GRAFTON

My stubborness prevented me from yielding to warnings to stay until my wounds had healed, and I hadn't ridden far before I realized the warnings had a lot of validity in them. My bandages were blood-soaked as my wounds had begun bleeding again from the pressure I had been putting on my arms as I leaned on my bicycle handlebars. One of the barbed wire prongs had gotten me on the big vein that runs along inside the elbow joint and it didn't take much to start it bleeding again.

I rode as far as Grafton, just west of the Appalachian Mountains, before I packed it in for the day. I proceeded on to the police station and was given a cell for the night, but my sleep was continually interrupted throughout the night as the drunks were especially restless and noisy in a nearby cell.

WASHINGTON, D.C. (first to fifth night)

I started pedalling again this morning. I went as far as I could before the condition of my arms made it impossible to continue and then I caught a bus the last part of the trip into Washington, where I made a phone call to my brother Brent.

Big B. (Brent) met me at the bus depot and we went to his place just near the University of Maryland at College Park. After getting settled, having a late chicken dinner, and exchanging a few past experiences, I went to bed early to prepare for a long day of sightseeing and relaxing.

I became so relaxed, comfortable and secure in the five days that I was there, that bicycling off into the unknown was almost a ridiculous thought, and it was going to become more ridiculous the longer I stayed.

"... i'd rather make mistakes,
        and find out
      who i am ...
than make the mistake
        of being afraid,
    and always wonder
          'who am i'?"

My brother showed me his office at the university and his dedication to his studies in astrophysics was beyond my comprehension. I also spent the week canoeing, meeting people, looking at the university, going to bars, sightseeing, playing football, and talking with Big B. and his friends.

Finally it became the eve of departure and the butterflies I had the last night in Vancouver returned. I had a very restless and sleepless night.

NORFOLK

As I left Brent my lower lip fell with fear as I glumly looked off in the direction I was about to be heading. My knees started bothering me but luckily not nearly to the extent they had at the beginning of my trip.

It was a very long and boring day and I couldn't figure out for the life of me what I was doing this for, but I also knew in the back of my mind that it wouldn't be long before I was back into it and naturally stoned again.

> *"... my greatest fear*
> *is that i become afraid,*
> *because i listen*
> *to what others think*
> *i should be*
> *afraid of."*

GREENVILLE

I had a very long ride today, but I was anxious to reach Greenville in North Carolina as it was Friday night and I had heard that there was a very good college there.

By the time I arrived I had bugs covering me in every imaginable place, crawling all about the hair on my body but not able to escape. I headed directly for the campus dorms to see if it was possible to get a shower. I was not only offered a shower, but a room for the night as well. It soon became worth all the misery I went through as I met some really good people.

> " ... *i want you*
> *to be happy*
> *to see me* ...
>
> *but,*
> *i don't want you*
> *to need to see me*
> *for your happiness.*"

NEW BERN

After travelling well over a hundred miles yesterday, I slowed down considerably and in the middle of the afternoon I pulled into New Bern and went about looking for a place right away so that I could spend the evening relaxing at a movie.

CAROLINA BEACH

Stoned!! Today I was stoned like I've never been or ever imagined I could be and it was entirely based on nature and people. If I had to put it into one word it would have to be a big Wow!

The day actually started out badly and warnings given to me about the dangers in North and South Carolina and Georgia already seemd to be coming true, and I was told that it would get much tougher as I proceeded south. I was riding calmly along with my thoughts flashing back to Vancouver when all of a sudden I was stunned by a barrage of little white things. After the attack, the people, who I must admit would have been complimented on their accuracy by any baseball coach, sped off in their nearby automobile. At first I considered chasing them but when I realized the mismatch, I decided instead to head to a coin laundry where I could clean my clothes which were now covered in eggs! This little incident really put me on my toes and I hope that for the rest of my trip through the south I'm not in such a tense and nervous state. It doesn't make riding very enjoyable at all.

When I arrived in Wilmington I phoned my parents which was a real lift as I was feeling very lonely at the time. Then I tried to forget what had happened and just look at everything with a new and open mind.

After phoning my parents, I headed on to what became a real "dream city", Carolina Beach. The people must have thought I was completely "bonkers" as I approached with the biggest, widest smile, dropping my bicycle, ran over the hill, and leaped in the freezing water with all my clothes on. The waves, bigger than any I've seen before, threw me about, and after picking myself up off my butt from the shore, fully exhausted and returned to my bicycle where I was questioned by some of the local people, I'm sure to see if what they were seeing was real or not.

My energy had returned by the evening and I went to a small bar where there were about fifteen people dancing, watching, talking, or whatever they felt like doing. I happened to have felt like dancing and if I hadn't exhausted myself in the ocean, I certainly did on the dance floor.

The waitress invited me back to her place afterwards, where she and her boyfriend lived, to have a few beers and spend the night. At first I declined their offer as I wanted to sleep on the beach, but accepted after they assured me it was going to rain tonight.

GEORGETOWN

By the time I finished riding today I found myself in Georgetown, South Carolina, my fifteenth State.

I spent the night there at the home of a girl I met. She and her brother, her brother's friend, and myself, went down to the local surfing area, and it was the first time I had ever seen surfing except on TV. It was very exciting to watch the surfing, and also most interesting to watch the surfers when they were out of the water. It appeared to me that their attitudes were much like young skiiers and young tennis players. Their attitudes seem to be one of a cockiness or coolness, and an "in love with one's self" behaviour. Sometimes these people hopefully grow out of this and realize what they have is only a gift. It is a result of our society that people go into something to be better than others rather than to improve themselves.

CHARLESTON

When I arrived in Charleston I was immediately approached by a girl who assured me that hair anything longer than a crew-cut in Charleston was like going into a sword fight without a sword. I just couldn't imagine things being all that bad here or anywhere for that matter, but I wasn't in any mood tonight to find out if there was any truth in it or not, so I readily accepted her offer of staying the night with some friends of hers.

After meeting her friends, who treated me especially kindly, I still couldn't accept that people could be so ornery and close-minded, but they reminded me that the movie, "Easy Rider" had a lot of truth in it. I had seen the movie before I left, which was probably a bad thing, as it now left me "shaking in my adidas".

The people I stayed with told me that the boyfriend of the girl that helped me was a real "greaser" and what she did for me would be very much disliked by him. I sure wasn't going to tell him.

JACKSONVILLE

I rode as much as I could today as I knew that
Florida was only a short distance away, and not only
would it be a thrill to enter, but also the Florida
coast was reputed to be a most beautiful ride. After
passing on through Savannah, Georgia, I continued on
until it was dark and the rain was by now coming down
heavily. I stopped at a roadside cafe to dry off and
to figure out where I was going to spent the night.
I was well past Savannah and about an equal distance
away from Brunswick. While I was sitting at one of
the tables in the cafe, obviously with a sad and con-
fused look on my face, a man came over and joined me
and questioned the reason for my glum look. I learned
from him that he worked for a trucking company. He
was presently heading all the way down to Miami and
offered me a ride. I told him that although it was
extremely tempting, I could only accept the ride to
Jacksonville, on the northern border of Florida. We
passed through Brunswick and shortly we entered
Florida and Jacksonville.

Here I ran into more friendly people who invited
me to their place to listen to records, and they let
me use the chesterfield for the night.

Before going to bed with all the roaches and
bugs that crawled everywhere, I shaved off my beard
that was very itchy due to the humid climate. As I
climbed into bed, I cringed at the thought of these
little animals crawling all over my sleeping body,
but then I realized that I was the intruder and if
they could put up with me, then to accept their presence was all I could to, though I know I would have
slept easier without them.

DAYTONA BEACH

It was obviously the weekend in this little
ocean-side town of Daytona Beach. The evening fes-
tivities were just beginning as I arrived and I decided I would head directly for the centre of all the

action which just happened to be a dance in a building near the middle of the town. The few conversations I did manage to overhear were about the latest drug busts and I was further depressed to see so many empty faces whose desire for, and interest in life seemed to be nonexistent.

COCOA

Just as I was leaving Daytona Beach I had the thrill of coming across the man, horse and dog that I had heard so much about who were attempting to go around the world. I knew they weren't too far ahead of me, but I never really thought I would ever see them. They were resting under the shadow of a tree before continuing their journey down south. He told me that they had come from Alaska. Bicycling is a slow mode of transportation in relationship to modern means of travel, but horse-back is many times slower. Bicycling would be the slowest way that I would ever travel a long distance. Besides, on a bicycle you do your own work and therefore you can alter your speed depending on how you feel. On a horse the speed is very regular.

WEST PALM BEACH

I made my way into West Palm Beach after a frustrating day of two flat tires within about fifteen minutes of each other. I learned from the local residents that flat tires were very common here as the area is well supplied with little "sand spurs". However, I don't think that I will have to worry too much about them as this may possibly have been my last riding day, as I hoped that I would be able to find work on a ship going from here to the West Indies.

First, though, I went into a newspaper office as I had promised my parents that I would send a clipping home when I had completed my trip. I was in for more than I had expected, however, as they became so interested in the trip that they even invited the mayor over to the newspaper office for the picture. I was told also that it was impossible to get work on a ship that left from here, but I was encouraged when they said that I would probably have more luck down south, so I knew that I had at least one more riding day ahead of me.

MIAMI

Today went quite smoothly as far as bicycling goes. The sun welcomed me to Miami but as was typical of big cities I was nervous and fearful of what lay ahead. It was late in the afternoon so I decided to postpone until tomorrow my visit to the shipyards where I hoped to be able to get a job on a freighter going to the West Indies. My thoughts were on the present moment and what I should do. It has been my experience up to now that the safest place in a big city is a university, so I promptly headed for the University of Miami, which was well on the other side of the city. This gave me a chance to see Miami and it also gave the motorists a chance to make nasty honks at me - a well-earned release of tension after a frustrating day at the office. It was some consolation to me that now they may be more pleasant to their families when they arrived home.

I went skinny dipping with some friends in a nearby lake late in the warm moon-lit evening. I really enjoyed it, although we were there on a night when the mosquitos were especially hungry. It was a weekend and this is probably the time when the most swimmers come. After a week without blood, the mosquitos go crazy!

Sunday afternoon I went to an outdoor concert. There is nothing like a concert when it's hot and sunny and it was hot and sunny today, so there is nothing like today.

I left early the next morning after receiving gifts of wrist bands and beads, and fortunately a good luck coin. I say, fortunately, because I was heading for the southern States where they look down on that type of apparel that I'm wearing and therefore I will probably require all the luck I can get.

NAPLES

I went through the famous Everglades today. About one hundred and ten miles of road that doesn't have the slightest twist or turn. Thank goodness the world is round. If I had been able to see the other end I don't think I would have made it.

I've heard many scary stories about the Everglades. There are bushes all along the sides and I could just picture snakes swinging from the trees like in the Amazon in South America, or tigers darting out of the bushes as in Africa.

After riding eighty miles which seemed more like 300 miles, I stopped at a restaurant. I was very thankful for this restaurant as it was getting dark, I had no light and there was no way I was going to spend the night on the side of the road. I met a very considerate person at the restaurant. He was English, about 45 years old, and very depressed. He did everything he could for me. He drove me to Naples which was about thirty miles, took me into a bar and bought me a drink, then proceeded to go around to different people in the bar telling them of my predicament. I insisted that I would be alright but he still continued his search for a good soul. The fact was nobody liked my shaggy look as a few of them were quick to mention. The English fellow said that I could have stayed at his place but he lived with a schizophrenic and the state of this person made it impossible to have visitors. It really hurts me to see unhappy people but I was especially sad to see such a good person unhappy. He worked on a yacht and hated his work. When I asked him why he didn't look for some other kind of work he replied that he would be unhappy whatever kind of work he did. Farewells do not get easier with the number of times you make them.

PUNTA GORDA

This was one of those days where you just want to
sell your bike and fly home. The road I travelled on
was very narrow and this resulted in many close calls
from cars and trucks. I arrived at Punta Gorda just
in time to see the sun going down. I received a lot
of dirty looks. One didn't have to be too perceptive
to get the feeling that you weren't wanted. Fortunately, one of the restaurants didn't realize I was
coming for they had a sign that read, "All you can eat
for $1.25". If the towns' people didn't want to run
me out of their town, the restaurant owner surely did
now. I have an unbelievable appetite. I have been
burning up energy instead of gas, and the money people
think I save on gas by travelling in this method only
goes towards food.

SARASOTA

On the way to Sarasota I stopped at a beautiful
beach in a little town called Venice. I had a swim,
mailed a few letters and then continued my journey.
It was very difficult to leave the beach, as I knew
this would be about the last chance I would get to swim
for a long while.

I found that the people here were extremely open
in their conversation. In this way they could air
their frustrations which are otherwise often repres-
sed and lead to an anxious and tense person, who is
afraid to show or express his true feelings.

TAMPA

I'm at the University of Southern Florida after
one of my most enjoyable rides. It was a beautiful
sunny day and I rode along with a big grin from ear to
ear. I got completely into bicycle riding today. I
guess it had a lot to do with the fact that many of
the people I met in Sarasota were going up to Tampa for
a peace march and I planned on meeting them there.

As it turned out, I missed the peace march by about fifteen minutes and therefore also missed my friends. This was a big disappointment for me and so I headed for the university. The campus was large but there were few people around as it was Saturday afternoon. The first thing I saw were two girls freaking out after taking acid - one wanted to kill the other. They were running around screaming with no idea where they were. I did all I could, which seemed to be nothing. They finally left and I was left with an empty, useless feeling.

I read a really good cartoon in "Mad Magazine" which sort of summed up a lot of my feelings. A hippie yells out to the cops: "fascist pigs!". A guy starts beating up the hippie. The hippie calls out: "Help! Police!". The police say to each other: "There's nobody here but us fascist pigs".

APALACHICOLA

Instead of taking the shorter route to Panama City, I decided to take the route that would take me down by the Gulf of Mexico then back up to Panama City. It doesn't take long for me to miss the ocean especially when the south is making me so tense and I really need to relax.

I got into Apalachicola around 3:30 p.m. and was at a store contemplating whether or not I should try and make Port St. Joe before dark. Apalachicola was very small and, judging from the looks I was get-ting, was quite down on longhairs. The prospect of spending the night here frightened me, although I'm sure that Port St. Joe would have been no better. My worries were soon solved, however, when a carload of school kids pulled up to the small store. They began asking questions about my trip when one of them, whose father was a minister, invited me to stay at their place. He didn't have to twist me arm as I readily accepted the invitation. If the entire town had the friendliness of these kids then I would have felt very badly about my first impression of

Apalachicola. As it turned out, from the people I
talked to, my first impression was a valid one. We
had a wonderful dinner followed by a relaxing evening with good conversation and discussion.

PANAMA CITY

I got up early so I could say good-bye to my
friends who had to go to school, and then headed off
towards Panama City.

I went to the campus cafeteria in Panama City.
It was empty except for one table where there was a
group of people playing cards. They invited me over
for a hot chocolate, found me a place to stay, and
then invited me to a party that night. I stayed at a
girl's home which overlooked the Gulf of Mexico. The
whole side of the housing facing the sea was plate-
glass windows. The patio had been torn away by a re-
cent storm so that you could look straight down for
about fifteen or twenty feet. The house seemed sus-
pended in air. It was a clear evening with moonlight.
I only wish I could take that whole scene home with me.
When I wake up in the morning I better not look out the
window again. I'll just pretend I had a beautiful
dream otherwise I don't think I will be able to continue my trip.

At the party quite a few people thought I might
have been a "narc" (narcotic agent). This feeling has
occurred often when Ihave stayed with people who smoke
grass or take other kinds of drugs. The reason is
that the punishment for the possession of drugs is
much greater than in Canada. The result is naturally a distrust of strangers and often even a distrust
of their own friends. This makes things understand-
ably cold at times which is a very sad situation.
This has occurred so frequently that I would just
simply leave for awhile to prevent an uneasy and
uncomfortable situation.

MOBILE

Just as I got into Mobile a van full of people pulled up beside me and invited me to their place for a fish and steak dinner. After dinner I pedalled out to the University in the pitch dark without any lights. It was extremely dangerous as the road was very busy.

I'm glad, however, that I took the chance as it turned out well worth my while. At Springhill College - a small Catholic college - I went to the college centre where I met a group of fun-loving people who were in an especially jovial mood, being a Friday night. After they showed me to a room in the dorms where I could stay, we all went to some very deep and meaningful plays.

GULFPORT

Well, this is the Mississippi I've heard so much about. Luckily I'm riding through at a narrow part of the States and by tomorrow I will be in Louisiana.

Today was particularly dangerous for riding. The highway was very narrow and the heavy traffic seemed to be playing a game to see how close they could get to me without hitting me. I phoned my parents today but didn't tell them of the dangers as it would only add to the worries they had already about me travelling by bicycle.

I stayed at a guy's place and he made me the most delicious dinner. We went out to a local pub with two other guys who were staying there. There were girls there from a local girls' college - they were apparently spoiled girls sent there because it was highclass. From what I was told the result was a plastic bunch of beauties.

One of the guys told me about getting thrown in jail for talking to a little Black boy. He was told that he couldn't talk to a Black unless he owned them. Is this really 1970?

NEW ORLEANS

This, I am sure, was my worst day of the whole
trip. The guys I was staying with got up early to go
to work. When I got up an hour or so later I was
greeted by a plain-clothes cop. The lady who owned the
house wanted to get rid of her tenant, my host, and
used the reason that she rented the house only to one
person. (It's too bad such people discourage others
from being good and hospitable). Anyway, she said I
was trespassing so the cop was taking me down to the
police station on the charge of trespassing and va-
grancy. He asked me if I had ever heard the word
"grass". I said that if he was talking about mari-
juana, then I had heard the word. He then asked me if
I had smoked any, and after some pretty quick thinking
I replied that I hadn't. Then I followed him on my
bicycle down to the station.

Finally, after they were all ready to throw me in
the klink for five days, I was able to talk my way out
of it. The cop, whose name I won't mention, although
he wrote it down so that I'd be sure to spell it right
in my book, was the most prejudiced, hate-filled, and
power-hungry individual I've ever met.

The next thing that happened was my flag got
caught in my gear system and ruined it. I had made a
Canadian flag with a felt pen and cloth hoping that
people wouldn't think I was an American skipping the
draft. Anyway, when it rained, the cloth got soaked
and instead of flapping in the breeze, it drooped down
and got tangled up with my gears. I had to go the rest
of the day in a low gear and even that kept slipping.

Next, one of the straps on my duffle bag broke
and this made riding more difficult. I was carrying a
lot of weight on my back which kept falling off to one
side of my body and this made balancing very difficult
as well as the discomfort of the weight all on one
side.

Three trucks almost hit me. One actually forced

me to go flying off the highway into the bushes.

As I finally got to New Orleans I had many nasty things yelled at me as well as the standard dirty looks - a very discouraging greeting to a city that I had looked forward so much to seeing.

LAFAYETTE

Today started out like one of those days where you think everything is going to go wrong. I was almost hit several times by cars as I travelled along. It began to pour and a Black fellow and an older white person, about 40 years old, who was wearing a wig, picked me up and offered me a ride to shelter. They were really scary and both were fairly big. The white guy began calling me names and was becoming very antagonistic. I got out in the pouring rain and continued my riding as anything was better than being in their truck.

By the time I got to the university the rain was coming down hard and I went into the cafeteria to dry off. A guy who worked in the cafeteria offered me a place to stay and after I had gotten cleaned up we went to a place called the "Peaceful Village". I met the greatest group of people there. Phil, whose father ran the place where people danced, played pool, or whatever, invited me to stay an extra night at his place where they were having a Sunday dinner of frogs' legs. He also promised me a hair wash at his wife's hairdressing school.

There is much French spoken in this area of Louisiana as it is made up mainly of Acadians who came down from Canada many years ago. The people were especially friendly to me when they saw my Canadian flag.

Phil and his friends were the strangest mixture of people. Their occupations and ideas were very different and yet they got along well together. They accepted and respected each other's way of life. Phil and Nat both had wives and went to college at USL.

Another friend worked as a narcotics agent. Another fellow I met worked for the CIA - a branch of the government where he was sent around the country to deal with spies, underground people and the like. They pointed out a fellow at the chicken place who used to work for Al Capone. After Capone died he went to Louisiana to hide and started a bootlegging thing. Then he became a bookie. This was a wide assortment of interesting people!

LAKE CHARLES

This beautiful day began early as I was very anxious to hit the road again although the thought of leaving these people was a sad one for me. Phil gave me some sandwiches and candies to keep my stomach happy for awhile. After only twenty miles a young guy on his way home from church invited me to his uncle's farm for lunch.   His little cousins told me all about the snakes in the area while we ate our hot dogs.

It was dark by the time I got to the college at McNeese. The atmosphere was unlike what I had been experiencing all day, but I did, however, meet a fellow who said I could stay at the Wesley Methodist Centre. It turned out that he was president of the student body and he invited me for breakfast at the student centre the next morning before I was on my way.

BEAUMONT

After breakfast I headed out of town towards the freeway. It was illegal to take a bicycle on the freeway but it was a very short stretch before I got to a side road that ran parallel to the freeway.

When I was passing through Sulphur I heard some people behind me yelling for me to stop. I turned around to see some older people bouncing up and down, frantically waving their arms and motioning me to come back. At first I thought it was trouble again, but things have been going unbelievably well the last few days and it was probably people who just wanted to give me more hassle. But after stopping I could see by their smiles that their intentions were friendly so I went back to see what all the crazy arm-waving was about. It turned out that they were from the local newspaper and one of the fellows had seen my Canadian flag when he has passed me on his way to work. They took a picture for the paper and then one of the writers, Mrs. Watt, did a very flattering story on my trip.

It was very unusual to see older people so friendly to longhairs, especially in an area where long hair was very uncommon.

Although quite cold, it was sunny which made the day very pleasant for riding. There were a few tense moments, however, like the close calls with the snakes, the near loss of life from the wild traffic when I had to go on the freeway for about twenty miles. I've had quite a few races with dogs actually and up to now I have been able to out-race them. I never realized bicycles could go so fast but when I get scared and the old adrenalin begins to flow I get a lot of surprised looks when I go whizzing past cars. I hope I never meet a determined dog as I'm not able to maintain this pace for a substantial length of time. It's really bad when another dog comes whipping out just when the first one gives up.

HOUSTON

I rode ninety miles to Houston today. Whenever I go in to a place that has been commemorated in song I find myself merrily riding along singing as loud as I can, "Going to Houston", "Way Down Upon the Swanee River", etc.

I learned a lot about snakes today and as a result my riding became less dangerous. The reason my

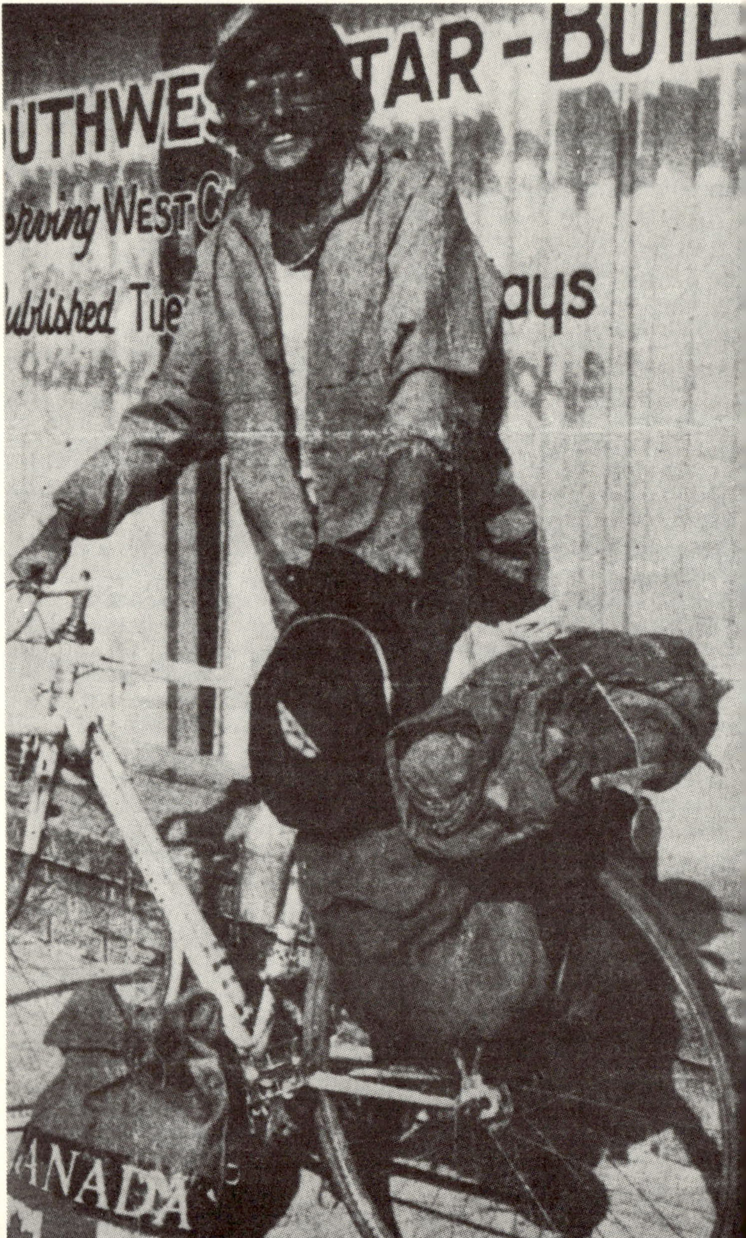
UTHWES TAR - BUI
erving WEST C
ublished Tue ays
ANADA

riding improved was that I rode down the side of the road, instead of down the middle line. I had always visioned big snakes leaping at me from the grass at the road. Then somebody told me that they can only strike at two-thirds of their body length. Also, un- like people, they only attack if they think their life is in danger. People are the only animals who kill for the sport of it.

The last little way to Houston was against a strong wind that made riding difficult.

After passing up an offer by a prostitute who was already very visibly pregnant, I found myself in an area of Houston that was really having a moment of excitement. Somebody had just shot a policeman and everybody was running around like crazy.

PORT LAVACA

I stopped at a gas station in Blessing around 2:30 after having ridden 100 miles today with another 35 miles ahead before I got to Port Lavaca. I made my favorite meal of peanut butter sandwiches before con- tinuing. The people at the station were very nice, but others in the distance were staring, laughing, and pointing. I told the attendants they should charge people 10 cents a look.

After nine hours of riding I made it to Port Lavaca, which was a little fishing town made up of about 85% Mexicans. I found the people very friend- ly, which really excited me about going to Mexico. My thoughts of going there weren't very definite up to this point.

The local police said that I could stay in one of their old cells. It wasn't like the other cells I have stayed in. Instead of bars it just had four cement walls. I dreaded the thought of them forget- ting that I was there. They took my fingerprints and my picture with a number around my neck - for the records, they said. One of the officers offered me

dinner at his house tomorrow night, but unfortunately
I planned on getting on the road, so I passed up his
invitation.

CORPUS CHRISTI

The first thing I did in Corpus Christi was to
go to the Post Office, the most looked forward to
thing on my trip, as this was one of the places I
received mail by General Delivery. I sat in front
reading my mail, disappointed that some I had expected
didn't come and I probably now wouldn't ever see, and
delighted with those that did come.

ROMA (U.S. side of the U.S./Mexican Border)

This was a very uneventful day as far as meeting
people was concerned but it was one of my most enjoyable and by far my longest ride of the trip. I covered 200 miles in only twelve hours from 8:00 a.m. to
8:00 p.m. The reason for the good mileage was due to
the strong wind at my back - which really was a change.
The first three hours I was doing between 25 and 30
miles an hour which was exceptionally fast considering
all the weight I carry. I didn't realize I was being
followed until an older man pulled off the road up
ahead, got out of his car, and motioned for me to stop.
He told me that he had been following me for quite a
ways and I had been averaging 30 miles an hour. This
showed me just how strong the wind was as I usually
average between 10 and 15 miles an hour over the whole
day, counting short little stops. In an average 6 to
8 hour day of riding I usually take only two or three
breaks of around fifteen or twenty minutes each.
Otherwise the only time I stop is to go to the bathroom or to fill my water jug.

I am sure I took the long roads to Roma and I am
never happy about doing unnecessary miles. I was riding along a deserted desert road most of the way and
was very surprised when I saw a car. One carload of
people even gave me a beer while I was pedalling

along. It came at a perfect time as my water jug
was empty and I was so thirsty I was sure that it
was all over for me.

I went the last two hours down a pitch black
country road. That was two hours by a watch anyway.
It seemed like days to me and I was just petrified
the entire distance.

I even had a big cow running along just ahead
of me. She was sure I was chasing her. I was ter-
rified when I first heard her but couldn't see her.
I only knew it was big as its feet fell heavily on
the ground. I was sure at first it was going to attack me and this was going to be the end of my journey. There was a fence running alongside the road
and she made many unsuccessful tries to crash through
it before she finally found an opening.

When I got to Roma I went to a gas station/
grocery store and bought myself a chocolate bar.
The two girls who worked there were very understanding of my condition and phoned the local pastor.
Although I felt like having him say a prayer over
what seemed like my last living hours, he didn't
think it was necessary and instead he put me up in
an old rectory which was no longer being used.
Goodnight.

LAREDO (U.S. side of the border)

And so ended one of my most frustrating days on
the entire trip. After peanut butter sandwiches for
breakfast, I rode over to the border crossing to
Roma. They told me there that I needed $50 a day to
get in to Mexico. I talked to everyone I could find
and I was getting angry as my words were falling on
deaf ears. The feeling I had from riding all the way
and then hearing people casually and without interest
say, "No, you can't go across". If they gave me a
reason I may have been more apt to accept it, but
when they give a phoney reason it is really hard to
take. Few people have enough money for $50 a day.

I have never been so close to hitting anybody, but I am sure this is what they wanted so they could throw me in jail and throw away the key.

When I finally gave up hope I decided that I had better try another crossing about twenty or thirty miles down the road. I received the same reaction there. I had been told that they don't let people with long hair into Mexico anymore, but they never come right out and tell you this. Also, shorts are not worn anywhere in Mexico except at tourist places on the ocean. I even tried to pay my way across as I heard that this was what the Mexicans expected, but the results were the same.

I met a Spanish-American who drove me in his car to two more border crossings and even with his help (he could speak Spanish to them as they often had trouble understanding English), I was met with the same reaction. It was Saturday now and I was going to have to wait until Monday to go to the Mexican Consulate in Laredo to see if I could get in. But first I was going to have to cut my hair. I am even questioning the fact of whether I really want to go to Mexico. If this is any indication of what it is like, then it will be the most miserable time. I have often heard that you can't judge Mexico by the border towns and you can't judge people by the border police. I hope they're right. Apparently the roads aren't all that suitable for riding bicycle which is also very discouraging information.

My nerves were getting very bad at this point so I went into a park to relax. I met a group of about eight young Spanish-American girls. Their happy, fresh smiles gave me a lift at a time when I was feeling like all was lost. Mexican girls have beautiful skin and features.

I checked all the hotels in town and they were either too expensive, or full up - though many times I felt they would rather just do without my business. Finally, I went to a large house that I thought was

the one somebody had told me about that rented out
rooms for the night. My directions were wrong but I
was sure glad they were. A couple of guys stayed there
and one of their girlfriends was down from Dallas for
the weekend and she had come with two of her friends.
That made it three guys and three girls!

LAREDO (second night)

I spent the entire day relaxing and drawing in the
park. Some girls cut my hair really short and my head
looked like a bowl when they finished. It's amazing
but depressing to think that now that I had my hair cut
I can get into Mexico although I am still the same
person.

I went to sleep to the sound of mice and bats.

> " ... *when we're children,*
> *we have*
> *limitless imaginations* ...
>
> *when we grow up,*
> *we are often limited*
> *by our image.*"

MONTERREY

This was a very interesting day mainly because
it was my first time in Mexico. I had three tacos,
then went to the Consulate where I had no trouble getting a visa. I crossed the border without any problems,
no doubt because I was this completely different person
who is now automatically acceptable.

I rode 100 miles through freezing cold and mountainous desert. What I've feared for a long time happened. I was riding along with my head down, daydreaming and thinking about friends back home. I looked up
just in time to see a big black stick on my side of the
road. But when it started wiggling it didn't take me
long to figure out that it was a snake. I completely
froze. I had one hand on my brakes and the other, I

think, was writing out my will. Instead of swerving
around him, I stopped about one foot in front of him.
If he didn't think he was being attacked now, I don't
know when he would ever consider that someone was at-
tacking him. However, instead of striking at me we
just looked at each other for a few seconds before he
decided to wriggle off the road into the grass. He
must have gotten vibrations that I was frightened to
death and that I didn't have harmful intentions. I was
sure that this was one of those deadly moccasins that
I've heard so much about and told that I would be very
wise to avoid if I was allowed a choice. Anyway, I
was shaking for the next few hours.

Only an hour after I had seen the snake, a wolf
passed across the road only about 20 feet in front of
me. I hope running into these scary animals doesn't
become a daily procedure.

I took the bus the last 40 - 50 miles into
Monterrey as there was no way I was going to sleep out
after the things I had seen today. Besides I still
didn't know anything about Mexican people and therefore, wanted to get to a big city where I would feel
safer.

The bus trip was really interesting. I was the
only one who couldn't speak Spanish - not even one
word, and the Mexicans are very different in appearance having a dark complexion and dark hair. I have
fair skin with sun-bleached hair. I tried to avoid
stares of curiosity by sitting in the back of the bus
but this didn't stop the people from turning around
and taking long looks at their unusual companion.
They would be sorry by tonight when the kinks in
their necks started to tighten up.

I was very shocked at first at the appearance of
Monterrey. They didn't seem to have any concern for
health judging from the garbage on the streets and
the pollution in the air. But the people were extremely friendly, waving and saying "hello" (ole!)
in Mexican, which was the first Mexican word I had

learned. I couldn't find anybody who spoke English
until I got to a university which specialized in psychology and philosophy. This was about the best
reception I've ever had which made me feel unbelievably good after my skepticism about finding happiness
in Mexico. I must have had a crowd of about 25 people
around me, none of whom could speak English but were
great company just because of their extreme warmth.
Finally, a few men who had learned of my arrival
and who could speak a bit of broken English, joined
our happy group. One guy, who invited me to stay
the night at his place, translated while the others
fired questions at me. After dinner I went for a few
drinks with the guy I was staying with and two of his
friends and their wives. One taught at the university and the other was student president. Neither,
however, could speak English.

MONTERREY

I decided to stay an extra day so when Gonzola
(I'm not sure how his name is spelled) got up early to
go to work, I slept in a couple of extra hours. When
I finally was able to drag myself out of bed I found
that Gonzola had accidentally locked me in the house.
The only possible way that I could get outside was
down a fragile pipe from the back verandah. It was a
second storey apartment that was more like a third
storey apartment compared to those in the States and
Canada. I wasn't sure the pipe was going to hold me
and I could just see the police waiting for me at the
bottom. The houses are all very close together and I
was sure people were going to think I was a burglar.
It was going to be very hard to explain especially
when I couldn't speak Spanish and I didn't know where
to find Gonzola. Eventually I took a chance on the
pipe and slid down.

SALTILLO

This was an amazing day all round. I took off
towards Saltillo at 7:30 in the morning when it was

below freezing, and during the day it got up as high as 75 degrees. I only rode 60 miles today which is actually a short riding day as I usually ride 80 or more miles, but it was all mountains. I went up over 3,000 feet.

The people on the way were exceptionally friendly and when I stopped at a gas station 12 miles out of Saltillo they actually came running over to offer me cokes. Although the people were very poor it meant more to them as I didn't have a cent in my pocket. I only had a postal money order and the only place I could get it cashed was in a bank in Saltillo. I was very hungry and the bank closed at 12:00 so I rode without really stopping from 7:30 until 12:15. I was 15 minutes late but I was relieved to find that the banks actually stayed open until 1:00 p.m. I went to three banks before I got my money. It was really frustrating to be weak from hunger, not able to speak Spanish, and then find out that I had to try another bank and go through the same routine over and over before I could get my money. The first thing I did was go to a restaurant. While I was trying to eat, everyone gathered around, staring. I am sure they were quite surprised to see that I, too, ate with my mouth. Then a newspaper man came over for a picture and story and although nobody else was fluent in English there were a few people who did their best interpreting. The story, as I learned from a Spanish-English student later, wasn't really the way I had told it, but it really didn't matter.

SAN ROBERTO

I stayed in a cheap hotel last night. Although my room was on the second floor, I carried my bicycle up the narrow stairs to my room. I have been warned about the amount of theivery in Mexico and I even take it into restaurants or leave it against the window outside and get a seat right next to the window.

My plans now are to continue on to Panama City, then to put my big toe into South America.

As I left Saltillo everybody was waving good-bye as they had recognized me from the article in the newspaper and had read of my adventures and future plans.

A highschool bus full of kids stopped and their teacher took a picture with them gathered around me. They offered me a bag of oranges, but I only took a couple. I could write a whole chapter on how good an orange tastes when you're riding along and your mouth is so dry that you can't even swallow.

I ate at a little restaurant just before I got to San Roberto. It was full of truckers and about six girls worked in the kitchen. One of the truckers gave me a brand new flashlight when he was leaving. This is something I need very much as I am often caught in the middle of nowhere when it is dark. It will be very useful I am sure. I asked the girls in the kitchen if they knew of any places where someone could crash. They all pointed at the best looking one. I said very casually that it was okay with me - I was trying to play hard to get but was having trouble covering my excitement. She very shyly told me no, that it was impossible. They did tell me that there should be somewhere to stay in San Roberto. I left after a great deal of talking with gestures and doing my best to throw in a few Spanish words.

It was dark when I got to San Roberto and the fellow said that I could sleep in the bus waiting room. It was very uncomfortable but it was better than with the snakes.

MATEHUALA

I got to Matehuala early - about 1:00 p.m. It was really hot so I went to a motel for a swim. Although I didn't plan on staying there they said it was alright for me to have a swim.

The little snotty-nosed, dirty-faced kids that hang around me do get to me at times, especially when there are a dozen curious little eyes staring at me when I'm trying to eat a meal. The owner tries to get them out so that I can enjoy the meal but his attempts are usually unsuccessful and I have pretty well accepted it now as an occupational hazard. I do have a great love for kids, but after a long day there are times when I like to be alone and relax and maybe just walk around unnoticed. This is impossible, however, except in a place where there is a lot of tourists.

SAN LUIS POTOSI

All the action yesterday didn't really start until well after I had finished writing and had gone to sleep. For about the third night in a row I had a lot of trouble getting to sleep as my nerves have been extremely bad and I am always on edge. Finally, however, I did get to sleep but in the middle of the night I had to get up and make a run for the bathroom. I was very, very sick. Incidentally I didn't make it as I flowed freely at both ends unable to control the mess I was making. When I first opened my eyes with the realization that I wasn't feeling too well, the four walls of my previously large room had closed right in on me. It was like being in a little box that started spinning. I remember thinking how much I wished I had someone there as I really felt like it was all over, but there was no one to turn to. I had a very lost feeling.

In the morning after I had cleaned up the mess, which was a difficult task considering my condition, I headed for the bus depot. I barely had enough strength to walk and my two-hour wait for the bus was interspersed with hurried visits to the washroom.

I took the bus a bit of the way to San Luis Potosi, but when I was feeling a bit better, I got out and started riding again. This was a definite mistake. I barely made it and by the time I was able to get across to people that I was looking for a doctor, I had almost

breathed my last. I had absolutely no strength.
The doctor actually had to give me a hand into his
office which was up only one stair. He gave me some
pills and it didn't take long before I was able to
get a grip on the situation again. The doctor could
speak a bit of English, and this and his warmth and
understanding helped just as much as the pills, I
think.

I didn't eat all day as I couldn't hold it down.
I found another cheap hotel and after a short rest I
went down to the market. The market was streets and
streets crowded with people and little stands carrying all sorts of goodies. There are many beggars in
the area, of all ages. If you give to these people
it doesn't take long for the news to spread and within minutes you have a whole crowd of kids with out-
stretched hands following you.

I bought a really good flute for only $3.20.

SAN LUIS POTOSI (Second night)

This was a quiet, uneventful day - I am feeling
much better right now.

I saw a soccer game, played my flute, and phoned
home. It was nice talking to my parents and I had
the most enjoyable surprise. Willie and Kips were at
my home when I phoned. It was really good to hear
their voices again.

QUERATERO

I got up with the sun this morning. Some
Canadians, from British Columbia yet, stopped me as
I was riding along. It turned out that they were
from Burnaby which is only about fifteen or twenty
miles from my home in West Vancouver. They gave the
the address where they were staying in a little town
on the other side of Mexico City.

I rode 135 miles today in eleven hours although I still haven't got all my strength back. When I got to Queratero a friendly policeman showed me to a hotel and gave me help in talking the price down from 30 pesos ($2.40) to 12 pesos (96 cents). Two alcoholics, as they informed me, invited me into their room for a drink of hard stuff. I am only a beer drinker and one glass of their mix and I was really flying. They kept trying to get me to drink more as they insisted that "we are all amigos here". But I wanted to look at the town so I told them I would come back later and join them. By the time I got back which wasn't very late, they had passed out so I quietly sneaked off to bed.

MEXICO CITY

I got up at 7:00 this morning and after starting out I climbed one of the steepest mountains I have ever seen. I then met a Mexican boy on a bicycle team who was out practicing. We rode together for some distance and although we had many questions to ask each other, we had much trouble communicating, but we both enjoyed the ride.

> *"... i may not always believe*
> *what you say and do ...*
> *but i can always say*
> *i do'believe in' you."*

When I rode into Mexico City I asked some people where the park was as I really needed the rest and relaxation before I dared venture into the city with its seven or eight million people. This was by far the most polluted city I have ever seen. The entire sky was red and I had much trouble breathing.

There was a little lake at the park. Water is soothing for my nerves and, although I prefer the ocean this was an appreciated substitute. The lake was packed with little rented rowboats and some young people invited me aboard their boat and we had the greatest time. I then headed into the big city to find a hotel. I still didn't have a place well after dark

and stopped to watch some Mexican dancers and met
some wonderful people.

I found a room for $2.40 and talked him down to
$1.20. There was barely room for the bed, let alone
my bicycle. I had to carry it with all its bags up
four flights of stairs. I will stay here a couple of
days as I want to get my bicycle fixed.

I got my bicycle fixed and got another set of
brake pads as well. After that I threaded my way
through traffic towards the university. I think that I
was going around in circles. I would ask people directions and I then find myself going in the wrong way.
Every street seems to be the main street and I've given
up the thought of looking for sights that I've heard
about that one should see. I would like to come back
here some day as it is definitely a very lively and
colorful city.

I spent the night sleeping on a floor. I have
been getting a terrible cold undoubtedly from lack of
sleep and nervous exhaustion.

This turned out to be a very interesting day.
After a fantastic breakfast I bade them all "adios".
I went to the television studio as a fellow told me
to go in there and see a fellow named Zabludovsky (?).
Zabludovsky asked me to go into his office where he
was surrounded by secretaries and other people - I
only noticed the secretaries. It turned out that this
man was one of the most prominent TV personalities in
all of Mexico. He asked me to come back tonight at
10:00 to go on his TV program "The 24-Hour Show". He
wanted me to wear my riding outfit and bring my bicycle.

I went to the studio early hoping to find somewhere to get a little rest. The television show turned
out to be a very exciting affair for me. The show is a
news and entertainment affair where guests are invited
and so I was on with ladies all dressed in their fan-
ciest clothes,and the men in their best suits. I had
on a pair of cut-offs, a pair of old running shoes that

were just barely hanging on my feet, a singlet, beads, a wrist band, and my newly acquired silver Aztec calendar. A girl interviewed me translating after I had answered her questions. During the show I received many phone calls and received offers of two hotels in Acapulco and one in Mexico City. This popular show was shown throughout Mexico City and apparently it doesn't even matter how poor the people are, they get a TV set before food.

I have become instantly famous in Mexico as I found out soon afterwards. If I wasn't pestered before, I had better get prepared for it now. The cartoonist on the show even drew a picture of me being chased on my bicycle by a policeman with a pair of clippers. I had told them of the trouble I had getting into the country because of my long locks.

I went directly to the hotel that was offered and planned on heading towards Acapulco.

CUERNAVACA

As I left Mexico City many people waved good-bye as I supposed they had seen the television show last night. It took me only three hours to travel 54 miles. The first half was up a mountain and I was really glad to have that over as I had heard the rest of the way to Cuernavaca was all downhill. The ride was a beautiful one as the mountainside was so fertile and green. I looked back at Mexico City from the top I could barely see the city because of the pollution. There was a line across the sky that showed how high up the pollution went. I was just barely above it.

Going down the other side of the mountain I must have been going at least forty or fifty miles an hour. This may not seem fast but if you consider being on a bicycle that feels every bump and every stone and the road is very windy, you will understand how I felt. I never really used my brakes as I never like to ride them, but then the worst thing on my whole trip happened.

Just before I got into Cuernavaca I put on my brakes. As I applied more and more pressure I was stunned when the brake pads just disappeared before my eyes. It quickly flashed through my mind that these were the new ones I had just gotten in Mexico City. I was very upset to say the least. My heart, I am sure, completely stopped while I was going through this traumatic experience. Cuernavaca is actually on the side of the hill and I knew I had to get stopped before I got there because death was certain if I went flying into town at this high speed. I started dragging my feet on the ground and rubbing my shoes against the wheel. Just before going down the final stretch into the city there was a flat stretch for about twenty yards. It was at this point that I swerved off the road into the bushes and am only thankful that I came out all in one piece, let alone alive. As I was hurtling down the mountain I was screaming at little kids to clear the road as they seemed to be waiting to cross just as I got there. I think this scare will remain in my mind for quite awhile and should make mountain riding very uneasy for me.

When it became dark I knew it was time to find myself a hotel. I ran into three young guys who had seen me on TV and they invited me to stay at their school. The padre and principal (the same person) said that I was welcome to stay the night. Classes were going on at the school until about 8:00 p.m. They have a very long school day and the principal asked me to come and talk to some of the classes. The rooms are really quite small but have about forty to fifty kids squeezed into them. It was actually my pleasure to go to the classes as the friendliness was beyond explanation. A couple of young people were volunteer teachers from the States and they translated as I told them a bit about my trip and then the kids asked me questions. Many of the kids shook my hand afterwards and the welcome feeling they gave me was overwhelming. I headed for the bathroom where I dried a few tears. The conditions were bad but the people didn't wander around complaining like most people do, myself included, when things aren't going right. I've really learned to appreciate little things as we only really need the necessities. Often luxuries make us forget about the things that are more important and meaningful in life.

That night the kids took me to a dance which was a fascinating affair. It is the custom to celebrate a girl's fifteenth birthday. The size of the affair depends on the wealth of the family involved. This family happened to be very wealthy and the result was a large formal affair.

We were let in free but I only stayed a little while as I had a long ride ahead of me.

TOXCA

Toxca is the most beautiful city I have ever seen. From its location it was such a feeling of satisfaction to look miles down and see the road I had taken winding up the mountainside. It has a church that I won't even try to explain. I can't even imagine the amount of work that was put in to it.

This just happened to be a big night in Toxca. A famous orchestra was in the church that evening to play Beethoven's Ninth Symphony which is my favorite piece. I heard about it too late and spent the rest of the night kicking myself. I did, however, have an enjoyable evening as I met many of the tourists who had passed me earlier in the buses. Our group invited me for a drink, another two couples invited me to stay at their hotel, another couple invited me for a meal when I got to Acapulco, and still another two older couples invited me to a nightclub show with the tour guide hostess. I declined the offer, not because I was playing hard to get, but because I was very tired and still had a very bad cold. Also, it was 175 miles to Acapulco and I wanted an early start as I desperately want to make it there by tomorrow.

ACAPULCO

I had about twenty hawks or vultures circling
above me today in the middle of nowhere. It didn't
really matter what they were because my thoughts went
to those animals in the desert and the vultures circling them before they die.

When I arrived in Acapulco many people seemed
to know that I was coming, as they had seen the TV
show and they showed me the way to one of the hotels
that I was offered. They were really spoiling me and
must have known how tired I was. They gave me a bed
that was wider than it was long, cleaned my clothes,
and kept my room tidy. This bed really beats ben-
ches and I really don't know how I'm going to leave
this place. I decided at this point that I was only
going to stay five days although the offer of the
hotel room was for longer, but I knew this was all I
could stay, otherwise I would have to make this the
end of my bicycle trip.

Before going to bed I went for a walk along
the beach and played my harmonica while the waves
sang their peaceful song.

> " ... *what i get*
> *most from you,*
> *is not what you*
> *give to me* ...
>
> ... *it's what i get*
> *from seeing*
> *how much you give*
> *to others.* "

ACAPULCO (fifth night)

I got up early to catch the early morning sun
and later I was joined by some girls I had met, and
we spent the entire day together.

In the evening about eight of us went to the
"L'Hourta" (whore house) which I found extremely

"... i was told i'd be
        'out-of-my-mind'
      to go after my dreams ...
  now that i've gotten out of my mind
            by following my heart...
        ... i'm living my dreams!"

interesting. I had heard that prostitution was big business in Mexico but I had no idea it was organized like this. There was an entire street with little bars on either side of it with prostitutes standing out in front. There were many older women there as well who were apparently mothers of some of the girls. I guess they were there to teach them some of their methods. At the end of this road was a big walled-in area with a bar and dance area in the middle. Around the outside were many rooms where the prostitutes and their catches went to do their thing. The traffic from the dance area to the rooms was very heavy although it always did seem faster in the direction of the rooms. There were many girls at this central area and they were definitely of a higher class than the ones in the streets. They roamed the dance area in their most tantalizing outfits and it was definitely good for a guy's ego to go there and have the girls hustling them for a change. The girls' motive was for money and the guys were there for sex and in the end both seemed to be happy temporarily - except for the girls who didn't get business and the guys who couldn't afford the girl of their choice. There were many people there who had seen me on TV and they threw questions at me such as "You do things like this as well as bicycling?" I tried to convince them that I was only observing, but judging by their smug smiles I knew I was not believed.

GLORIA

It was just beautiful to go to sleep last night to the sound of the waves slapping the sand just outside the front door. First on my agenda in the morning was a dip in the ocean so the salt water could clean out the poison those nasty little mosquitos put in my system.

I planned on staying another day at least but know I can't stay any longer if I don't want my bicycle sent home in a box. I say this because this is the most fantastic setting I have ever seen and would not find it very difficult to spend a long, long time

here. I will always keep it clear in my mind and hope
to come back, but my trip now has become too important
to pack up in the middle.

Tom and Gary, from Vancouver, and two fellows
from the States and I spent the light hours on the
beach surfing (body), playing soccer, throwing friz-
bies, chess, and hearts, and the dark hours (we had no
electricity) were spent playing bongos, talking, and
sleeping.

GLORIA (third night)

Today was spent in a similar manner as yesterday.
In the evening we went into town in Tom and Gary's van
to see a show. When we came out the van had been broken into and a stereo had been taken. I'm sure that
Mexicans learn in school how to break into vans as
everybody I have seen that owns a van seems to have
had it broken into at one time or another. It really
isn't hard to understand, however, as one of the
others pointed out, when you put yourself in the po-
sition of a starving Mexican and then you see tourists
flashing their money around.

OAXACA

I got up at 7:00 this morning and immediately
tried to get myself in a positive frame of mind for
my ride ahead.

It was a long, hot day and seemed hotter when I
sweated my way up many small hills. I just missed
another snake today. He was about as thick as an
average-sized arm (no exaggeration). I turned around
only to see him madly waving his fist at me. He does
not have a golden opportunity like this every day and
it might be a long time before he has another.

After riding for about ten hours and covering
around 140 miles, I had another flat tire. A truck
gave me a ride into a small town and after finding

out that the road from there to Oaxaca was impossible
to cross by car or bicycle, I threw my bicycle on the
back of an old rugged bus that was about the only
thing that was able to stand the bumpy rock and dirt
road. I was on the bus in my little cramped seat,
without hope of getting any sleep from 7:00 at night
until 7:00 the next morning. I was feeling very sick
by the time I arrived in Oaxaca and I became very upset when they charged me again for the transport of
my bicycle. The guy knew he had charged me twice but
knew he would get from me what he wanted as there
were many Federales within the immediate vicinity ea-
gerly waiting for some action.

TEHUANTEPEC

After I had my bicycle repaired I immediately
headed out towards Tehuantepec. It was difficult riding because of my tiredness and I will always regret
leaving Oaxaca so soon - a city I had heard so much
about.

> *"... the unconditional love*
>> *you have shown me*
>> *in a moment,*
>> *has shown me,*
>>> *that it is possible*
>>>> *to love,*
>>> *at every moment,*
>>> *under all conditions."*

The men here in the south, with their feelings
of superiority over women, often try to show off their
manliness in fighting. Tonight I thought I would

spare my life and rob them of an easy victory and
ego-booster by going to bed early. This is my first
sleep in a few days and I'm feeling very run-down. I
am the only "gringo" (American tourist) in this small
town and any new face is a delightful challenge after
an evening at one of the local bars.

ACAYUCAN

I just sat down on my bed in my $1.20 hotel room
and I honestly don't think I will be able to get up
again. I rode more than twelve hours, from 6:45 a.m.
to 7:15 p.m., through mountains and at times against
a fairly strong wind. In all I covered 150 long miles
with very few short breaks. I pedalled much harder
than on one of my average days as I knew I had to make
excellent time if I hoped to make it before dark, and
I really feared the dark as the road was extremely
dangerous even in the light of the day. When I finally did arrive, safely but exhausted, in Acayucan,
I am sure there couldn't have been a happier and more
relieved person in town. I celebrated by getting
about twelve hours of much-needed sleep.

All the stories I heard about banditos before I
came to Mexico, and that I thought were just make-
believe, are actually very true. Apparently they
killed five policemen who were up in the mountains
around Acapulco looking for them. And only a few
days before, a couple had been robbed and killed on
one of the nearby roads. I'm very scared about the
thought of a gang of them swooping down the mountainside and doing me in. Horses chasing a bicycle would
be a very novel idea for a TV show, but I could certainly do without it in real life.

COATZACOALAS

It is only noon but I don't know whether I will
be staying in Minititlan the night or not. It began
to pour with rain just before I arrived here and I
am presently sitting in a cafe browsing sadly through

my soaked belongings. By the looks of the dark sky this rain should keep up for days, but the people assure me that this is a common thing and it should be sunny and clear within the hour. I couldn't believe it when it was sunny and clear in only about half that time.

Coatzacoalas became my new destination for tonight's rest.

I honestly can't believe the rundown condition of the roads in the little towns in the southern part of Mexico. I'm sure they do a bad repair job on purpose so that they will always have a job, or else they have unimaginable hangovers when they do fix them. The traffic is at a crawl in most areas of the town or else their cars would be in complete ruin by the end of the day. As it is, I'm sure the life span of cars down here is very short. My bicycle has aged more in this stretch than anywhere else and I am continually having my wheel frames straightened. But worse of all my rear end is suffering a terrible beating.

It was 1:00 when I left for Coatzacoalas with my seat full of blisters and bruises. It was only 45 miles to Coatzacoalas plus the 26 miles I had done this morning, but the condition of the road made it a very uncomfortable 45 miles. I only hope that the road isn't like this all the way to Yucatan because there is no way that my bicycle will be able to stand it, let alone my posterior.

It was nice coming into a place fairly early and after booking into a hotel, I went over to the city square where I played basketball with some Mexicans. It was enjoyable to play a different sport for a change - a thing I really miss away from home.

My parents invited me to Hawaii for a rest at the beginning of February. This really gives me something to look forward to though I could handle another rest right now!

COATZACOALAS (seond night)

I've had a sudden change in plans, and instead of continuing on towards Yucatan I am now heading towards Veracruz, then inland back to Mexico City. The reason was that last night I had a replay of my night in Matehuala where I was so sick that I was sure it was all over. I was in the bathroom with my head drooped over the toilet most of the night. I think my condition was a result of the food, and general fatigue. I stayed in bed most of today as I was very weak and dizzy aside from my vomiting and diarrhea.

In the evening I went for a little walk before going to bed. I saw many groups of little children singing Christmas carols at people's doorsteps, chaperoned by a proud, smiling mother. I gave a happy cry and a desolate loneliness came over me. This was my first realization that Christmas was not far off and I was going to be spending it away from my family and friends. I became very homesick as my thoughts wandered to recollections of past Christmases.

> " ... *i learn most from you,*
> *not when you*
> *'try' to teach me ...*
>
> *but,*
> *when you 'are',*
> *what you want me*
> *to know.*"

CATEMACO

What a beautiful feeling - actually heading in the direction of my home in Vancouver! I know now the feeling horses get when they are heading home and why at this stage they start running faster. I am having a similar reaction on my bicycle and I will have to consciously slow myself. I planned on riding only about 45 miles to Coatzacoalas as this is my first day of riding after being sick but I had gotten up at 7:00 this morning and I was in Coatzacoalas by noon, and having nothing to do there I decided to push on towards Veracruz and the ocean again.

I ended up doing 110 miles and in one stretch I swear I was climbing a mountain for three straight hours. I was getting progressively weaker and was sure I was going to pass out on the side of the road at any moment. It didn't help when people told me that I still had a long way to climb. With a big sigh (more like a gasp) of relief I had finally made it to the top. By the time I had reached the top I was dearly looking forward to coasting down the other side. It was enjoyable as I thought it would be, but unfortunately it seemed to last only about ten minutes. Not only was it nice coasting down the mountain, but my view of Catemaco was just too much! The roadside and as far off into the distance as I could see was green and lush with a variety of trees and growth. Off on my right at the bottom of the mountain I could see a small lake which grew as I neared and little houses could be seen scattered around its edges though the trees hid many more. Little mounds of ground poked out of the water's surface and these little retreats could be reached by rowboat.

Being a Saturday night, I decided to go out to town. I really don't know the reason but things do seem to liven up on Friday and Saturday night. Actually my going out on the town entails just looking around and sight-seeing which I do in pretty well every town. I've therefore been going out on the town every night which is undoubtedly the reason why the weekend is no different to any other night. After a shower I put on my best pair of jeans, my best and only pair of moccasins, and my seoncd best shirt, as my best shirt was soiled from too many nights out on town. I then headed out for "el centro". The only action going on was a Spanish film at the only theatre so I ended up sitting on the edge of the sidewalk with a group of young kids. I bought them popcorn then walked back to my hotel along the side of the lake. The lake was very peaceful tonight. I wonder if it is more beautiful tonight only because it is a

Saturday night? I was in bed by 8:30 after a very action-packed Saturday night!

VERACRUZ

I rode 110 mountainous miles today and arrived in Veracruz just before dark. I only stopped a couple of times to grab something to eat. I never lack company at roadside cafes as there are always swarms of flies. They are the common black household fly that come in great quantities in Mexico.

After such a long day with many close calls on the narrow and dangerous road, I was ready for an early night. But after six unsuccessful attempts at finding a hotel with a vacancy, being the Christmas holidays and all, I had to settle for the L'Horta. This was the hotel where all the whores brought their evening visitors and my sleep was interrupted by many excited footsteps followed by what I gathered were satisfied departing footsteps. I had no fear of being lonely, however, as bugs crawled at their own leisure around the room that I had so kindly rented for them for the evening.

PUEBLA

I got up fairly early this morning as I wanted to buy new running shoes and razor blades and then spend the rest of the day lounging on the beach. I hadn't really gotten very much sleep due to all the action last night and so I wasn't feeling too chipper. Parting with my old shoes wasn't any easy task. They had come with me all the way from Vancouver and just to tell them that they were getting old and had served their purpose but were of no more use seemed like a very hard and cold task, but I knew I had to do it when people would only talk to me at shouting distance.

I arrived at the beach about 9:30, went for a swim, then planned to lie around and take it easy for the remainder of the day. However, by 10:30 it became very cloudy and the chance of it clearing again looked very slim. Therefore I got together with myself and we decided that to continue on towards Mexico City would be my wisest move. Unfortunately, this proved to be a very unwise move, and one that I was to regret. After I had gone only twenty miles out of Veracruz I had nothing above me but clear blue sky and a sun which gave off heat that just wouldn't quit. After fifty miles I became very weak and sick and also very disappointed that I had made such a wrong decision.

> "... *building walls around me*
> *takes energy,*
> *and i feel old and tired ...*
> *when i tire of building walls,*
> *i have lots of energy,*
> *and i feel young again!"*

Being sick has become a very common and therefore expected feature of my trip through Mexico. I usually just keep on pushing unless I have no strength at all and pedalling is impossible. Today was one of those days. The only thing I can do when this happens is to catch a ride into some place and hope that a nice long sleep will have me cured, at least temporarily.

Before stretching out for the night I decided to see a bit of Puebla, as with all the places I've been, I may never get a chance to see them again.

It was 2:00 before I got home and my thoughts of an early start to Mexico City were easily forgotten. I was asleep for only a little while when the fun started. If there was a 20-yard sprint from a lying start in the Olympics I am sure that I would win it hands down. I had the "trots" nine times in all during the night, and I'm sure by the morning I was down to around 75 pounds. At least my bicycle won't be carrying so much weight now. I am very anxious to get to Mexico City where I know a few people and will be able to take a few days off during Christmas. The rest is very important to me right now as my state of health has made me consider seriously the idea of just hopping a plane home.

MEXICO CITY (first night)

This is actually the morning after my first night in Mexico City as I was unable to write last night. I met a young Mexican fellow who could speak English, who realized that I was in desperate need of help, although I think he could see that from my expression alone. He told me that a couple of his amigos were heading for Mexico City and that he was sure I would be able to get a ride.

By the time the Mexicans and his amigos came along I'm sure that my head and body had gone their own separate but painful ways. I think they put my bicycle in the back of the truck, then helped me into the cab, although my recollection of even being alive at the time was very vague.

MEXICO CITY (second night)

I spent most of the day resting in bed. I was feeling a bit better although I was still fairly weak and dizzy and still made the occasional rush to the bathroom.

MEXICO CITY (third night)

I feel no better today and it doesn't look like I will be completely better for a long time. I phoned an American doctor in Mexico City and he prescribed some more medicine for me and told me that I definitely needed a long rest. It didn't take much to convince me as it is absolutely impossible to ride in this condition and if I did get better it would be only a short while before a recurrence would set in and, if it is possible to imagine, it would undoubtedly be worse. I then decided to take a bus to

Acapulco and spend January there and then fly to
Hawaii in February where I would meet my parents.
I would send my bicycle home by air freight.

I spent another uneventful day although I did
wash my clothes the old-fashioned way on the cement
blocks. This is strictly a woman's job in Mexico, so
all the ladies had quite a laugh when I joined them
at the old scrub board.

MEXICO CITY (fourth night - Christmas)

I've had another drastic change in plans. There
is no way that I can just quit my trip with only 3,000
more miles before I'm home. Besides, these will be
the best miles of the whole trip, up the beautiful
California and Oregon coasts. I am still very sick
but will keep my fingers crossed that this new pre-
scription works.

I just took it easy again today, although I could
get out of bed and spent a good part of the day down
at one of the squares.

I have really been avoiding people lately. I
just want to be alone. I suppose it's better I'm very
sad and homesick for Christmas in Vancouver, but I
think it's also because I'm not feeling well and everyone else seems so happy.

> " ... *i saw a group of blind people*
> *crossing the street,*
> *helping each other,*
> *laughing, &*
> *openly showing warm feelings*
> *towards each other ...*
> ... *they were all different*
> *ages, colors, & styles of dress ...*
> ... *it didn't seem to influence*
> *their caring for each other ...*
>
> ... *i couldn't help wondering*
> *'who' is really blind.*"

MEXICO CITY (fifth night)

I decided today that I was going to continue my bicycle trip north first thing tomorrow morning. The Mexican family looked at me as if I were completely bonkers when I told them of my plans, but I knew inside that this is what I have to do.

I went to the amusement park with the Mexican family and we had the greatest time even though I was too chicken to go on some of the rides.

When I got back to the apartment about 10:00 everyone wanted to go to a movie so it was about 1:00 before I got to bed. It's going to be hard getting up to ride tomorrow morning.

CELEYA

I left Mexico City about 9:30 and it really was a good feeling to be on the road again. I left the Mexican family a box of chocolates and a note but it seemed so little to give after all they had done for me. I rode about thirty miles in all before I got to the "cuota" (toll highway) from where I was going to have to catch a ride as bicycles weren't allowed on them.

I got a ride in a truck to Queratero and from there rode my bicycle 35 miles into Celeya.

LA PIEDAD

I went to breakfast first thing in the morning at the guy's house who had invited me last night. They were very friendly and hospitable and as typical of families in Mexico they had many children. I was treated to a large delicious dinner before the two youngest boys gave me an escort out of the city. I had to pedal like crazy to keep up with the little characters. It was sad saying good-bye to such a large and good family of eight kids, a mother, a father, pet rabbits, turtles and dogs. (Their pet crocodile had just recently died.)

I rode 100 miles today and the last twenty miles were in the dark, which never has, and I don't think ever will, add to my enjoyment of riding. As a matter of fact it usually leaves me with some very bad thoughts about riding which I was to experience again tonight when I had more close calls from those little power-run beasts. They are definitely a menace to my nerves if not a threat to my life.

> " ... when i'm confused ...
>
> ... it's better
>   to say what i'm feeling,
>   & have it sound confusing
>   to someone ...
>
> than to confuse someone
>   by waiting
>   until i can say it
>   better."

I met a real warm Mexican fellow about 45 years old, who took me to a public shower place. We were followed by many excited little footsteps obviously curious about this new arrival in town. The fellow kept his eye on my bicycle while I had the greatest shower. After the shower he was showing me to a hotel when two policemen called me over to their car. I remember thinking to myself at the time that it was all over for me and I would be spending the rest of my life in jail for no reason at all. It's just that I've heard so many terrible stories, undoubtedly exaggerated, about the Mexican police. I heard that if you get thrown in jail in Mexico your chances of ever being seen again are very slim, and often the offense is totally unknown. Anyway, I knew I wouldn't be able to get away on my bicycle, and my attempt of escape would only make things worse, so I took a big gulp and bravely walked over to the car. Fortunately, I misinterpreted their intentions, and, as a matter of fact, their reaction was completely opposite to the one I had expected. They, too, had seen me on the show in Mexico City, and along with many of the townspeople, escorted me to a hotel where one of the policemen treated me to a room and then took me in the police car to a cafe. He bought two dinners. Naturally, I thought one was for him and one was for me. I wondered while I was eating mine why he wasn't eating the other. When I finished mine, he gave it to me also. He had remembered me saying on TV that I ate a lot due to the fact that I burnt up so much energy. He had eaten just before I had gotten into town. He then drove me back to my hotel and we wished each other the best. It's too bad all law officers don't have such warmth and friendliness.

After my friend had left I went to my room to change before going out on one of my usual tour of the town. I bought some of my favorite food - peanuts with shells - and then went to a cine. I found a seat well away from the other people so that I could enjoy crunching my peanuts and after demolishing the whole bag, I staggered back to my hotel room with a nice set of cramps.

ZABOTLANEJO

It is only 7:30 in good old Zabotlanejo but I am already getting ready to hit the pit, for a good long sleep. I rode ninety miles today and no matter how many times I tell myself that I've got to slow down, I just can't.

The reason I am pushing hard is to get to the ocean which doesn't look that far on the map, though nothing ever does, and also to get to Tepic where I am hopefully expecting more mail. I have missed my last couple of mail places - Acapulco, because people thought I was going to get there later than I did, and Merida, because I ended up not going there.

The road was much better today which still does not mean it was very good (it wasn't), but yesterday my bicycle and rear end had to go through a lot of misery. Incidentally, there hasn't been any real improvement in my bottom's condition and I very much suspect that it was more than bruises that I had before. I only hope it isn't anything serious.

I said goodnight to all the flies that were swarming around my room, then pulled my blankets over my head so they couldn't have a party on my face while I tried to sleep.

AHUACATLAN

This little town is actually a little way off the highway I have been travelling and I'm sure, judging by the people's reactions, I was one of their first visitors from the north of Mexico. I even had people waiting outside of my hotel room hoping to get a quick peak at the freak.

It is only 7:00 right now, but I am getting very excited as in only one hour there is an Edgar Allan Poe scary movie at the local theatre for a mere one peso (eight cents). It just doesn't do poor Edgar justice. I left the theatre after about fifteen minutes when everyone began whistling and shouting back and forth to each other which made it impossible to hear what was happening. The picture was so old that I couldn't see what was happening either. I didn't even ask for my eight cents back.

The hotel room I got in Ahuacatlan is the biggest I've ever had, with two double beds, and all this for only 96 cents. This is really nice for a change as usually my room is only large enough for a single bed which means I have to sleep with my bicycle.

SANTA CRUZ

It was a most enjoyable day for riding and made me very optimistic about having a festive New Year's Eve.

It was only 35 miles to Santa Cruz and as I was already at the 3,000 foot level I naturally figured that the distance would be all downhill and should be fairly steep. I was wrong. About the first fifteen miles were all uphill, which meant that there was no chance of getting into Santa Cruz before dark, and the downhill was really steep.

Riding my brakes was impossible as they would have been worn out in no time and I wouldn't have had any when I needed them most. The result was a bicycle swerving down the mountainside at an incredibly high speed guided by a rider whose every little muscle was tight and tense with fear. My eyes watered freely and left me with a very blurry vision of this frantic episode. At one curve I spun out on the gravel and came within a hair of going over a cliff that went straight down for I-don't-even-want-to-remember how far. I pass the entire thing off as a real bad nightmare.

Well, my day just didn't go up and down, it went back up again and I was very happy to have such a great New Year's. When I finally got into Santa Cruz just after dark, I met an American fellow who had rented a small shack in this Mexican village for the winter and was doing some writing. He invited me to stay the night. There were a few younger people living on the beach who had come down from the States on their Christmas vacation to do some surfing. We had a very peaceful and relaxing New Year's, although we went to bed about 10:00 - a real late night for the others and myself as the weather is so beautiful that everybody always wants to get up with the sun.

SAN BLAS

First thing in the morning I took a little stroll in the village where I had spent the night. It was even more attractive than I could have pictured it from the description given to me last night.

After my short tour I headed back to the river to wash my clothes on the rocks so that they would be dry by the early afternoon for my ride to San Blas before dark. At the river was a Mexican lady whose physical appearance would frighten any man in the ring, but I'm sure her frame was big only so that she could carry her huge heart of gold. She was scrubbing away on her family's clothes with her two little daughters. She smiled warmly and I returned the greeting. Just before I settled down to the business at hand she took my clothes away and she and her daughters took over and did the most masterful job. I offered her money which she refused, but she accepted a soft drink for herself and her daughters. It took about an hour to drink these "pops" as our fits of happy laughter were a frequent interruption. I left with the happiest sadness and with a sore stomach from laughing so much.

After hanging my clothes up to dry, a group of about eight Mexicans ranging in age from ten to fifty, motioned me over to a small cement area where they were having a little soccer game. They had the same smiling, contented faces as the lady at the river.

One of the straps on my pack sack broke and a lady who lived in the village offered to sew it for me. She only charged me a few pennies for the materials.

By 2:00 my bags were all packed and I bid my friends farewell. I had to push my bicycle for about the first seven miles as the road was rocky and it would have ruined my wheel frames and aggravated my posterior some more - an inconvenience I can definitely do without as it is really bothering me now.

From here to San Blas, with the exception of one small stretch, I rode along the hard, sandy beach which totalled about twenty miles. It was really a beautiful scene as it was nearing evening time and I would watch the sun set as I pedalled merrily along. All was not beautiful, however, as something very unexpected happened to make things extremely miserable. Just as the sun was setting a signal was sent out to all the mosquitos in the area that it was time to go out and play. What I didn't realize was that I was going right into a swamp area where the mosquitos usually make their home. It soon became dark and I rode along, pumping as hard as I could, I could barely see because I had to keep my eyes closed as much as possible otherwise they would be filled with bugs. They found their way into my nose and ears, and even my mouth.

I finally did make it and after meeting some people and having a shower at their place I felt like a new man.

ESCUINAPA

A family I had met gave me a ride from San Blas up to the main road as this side road would have been hard on my bicycle. It was too far to the next town if I hadn't gotten this short ride. They offered me a ride all the way to Los Angeles and although it was really tempting I knew that I would never be able to forgive myself if I had taken it.

I got out of their van where I though I would be able to make Escuinapa by dark. I misjudged the distance and had to ride the last ten miles in the dark. Again, it wasn't lonely, as the bugs came out in large numbers and covered me from head to toe.

MAZATLAN

Just as I was coming into Mazatlan, I was faced with a heavy wind. I was looking forward to getting to Mazatlan - apparently a big tourist area - and this wind, which slowed me down to about three miles an hour, made me take two hours for the last six miles - about an hour and a half more than it should have.

I met a couple of Canadians on the beach - they were the only two other people there as most of the people felt, I suppose, that it would be smart to stay inside until the wind passed over. I went to the hotel where the Canadians were staying and the manager

gave me a room for a mere 80 cents. The two Canadians were paying $2.00 a night for their room so
were understandable upset. I wasn't going to complain,
however. I must look really down and out to get all
these deals - everybody must feel sorry for me.

Mazatlan has a beautiful location with small
cliffs and rocks that protrude out of the ocean making
a most fantastic picture. I don't really enjoy tourist towns, and this was a typical tourist town. The
local people are all out after tourists' money, and
the tourists don't really know what the natives of a
foreign country are like. They only see tourist-town
Mexicans. Theymay have a nice holiday, but they undoubtedly go home with a false impression of the Mexican people and Mexico.

> " ... *success is not*
> *what i do,*
> *& what others think*
> *about it ...*
>
> *sucoess is*
> *how i do it,*
> *& that i feel good*
> *in my heart*
> *about it.*"

CUILIACAN

I started out early this morning and was feeling
really sorry for myself. This state of mind is disas-
trous if I have any hope of enjoying riding today.

I can't believe the number and variety of dead
animals on the side of the roads throughout Mexico.
There seems to be little concern about it as the car-
cassess are left to disintegrate in even well-populated
areas.

Many people from Vancouver stopped today and they
were all friendly which made me even more excited to
get home. On the whole, tourists haven't been the

friendliest people and I'm quite sure the reason is
that they don't feel that one should travel until
he has retired or has his two-week holiday from work.
Then he has earned his temporary freedom. Many times
I have been asked, with obvious resentment, how I can
possibly work for three or four months in the summer
and then be able to afford to travel for the remainder of the year. Again, people are applying their
standards to somebody else. Everyone should have
the opportunity of making his own choice so long as
he isn't making it with the intention of using somebody else.

Anyway, the friendly people whom I met today
gave me a big lift and put me back in a good mood,
and I finished the day having ridden 120 miles. The
last twenty miles were really scary, however. After
100 miles it began getting dark; there were no signs
of any towns on my map. I was on the main highway;
I had no lights; I was hungry and thirsty; cars were
whizzing by within inches of wiping me out; there
were many bugs; snakes and scorpions were not uncommon; and a cold spell had hit this part of Mexico!
Sleeping on the roadside, however, was definitely
out, so I pushed on.

Finally, after I had ridden 120 miles I saw a
few lights well off in the distance. It took a long
time but I finally arrived at a few scattered shacks
which only had candles and fires as their means of
light. I was really nervous as I approached a group
of people sitting around a small fire. I had no idea
how they were going to react to my presence. Things
were going so bad right now, I don't know what I
would have done if they disapproved of their new vi-
sitor. Luckily this wasn't the case, and I couldn't
have asked for anything more in the entire world
than their warmth at this moment.   I explained
my situation in my still broken Spanish - I'm up to
about fifteen words now

LOS MOCHIS

I rode another 100 miles today, but this was an especially tough ride. It was freezing cold as a storm had come down from the north into the mid-west.

I had told myself beforehand that if I had gotten into this town before 3:00 I would stay put, as there was no way I wanted to ride at night again. It was pretty safe as I was quite sure I was going to arrive after 3:00. As it turned out I did, in fact, arrive after 3:00, but after I bought a chocolate bar I just kept on riding - oblivious to my earlier plans. Usually this would have been a mistake, but for once I had made a decision I will always remember as a good one.

I knew it was another race against the dark to reach Gusuave, and I will never know why I did it. After I had gone only ten miles, Tom and Gary, the two Vancouver guys whose shack I stayed in fifteen miles out of Acapulco, pulled off the road in front of me in their van. This was definitely one of the happiest moments of my life and there was no way we were going to pass up a celebration. They offered me a ride into Gusuave, but I told them I would meet them there in about an hour as I wanted to avoid cheating. It was a big mistake as the wind came up stronger then ever and I became very upset and frustrated as I wanted badly to get there. I finally did arrive and after riding through town and not finding a suitable pub, we decided just to throw my bicycle in the back of their van and go on to Los Mochis. Just as I was putting my bicycle in the van, the second unbelievable coincidence occurred. The family I had met in San Blas and had spent time with, and who had given me a ride to the main road and offered me a ride right to Los Angeles, pulled up beside us. The whole thing was simply unbelievable and we all met in Los Mochis, where we had a few drinks and all spent the night. I can't believe that any of this would have happened if I had stuck to my original plans. It certainly won't help to slow me down from now on. I'll always think that if I stop I will miss something like this happening again.

"THE MIDDLE OF NOWHERE"

It was 3:30 in the afternoon, I had ridden
fifty miles, and I was at a gas station in the middle of nowhere. A Mexican man that worked there
told me that he had some amigos that stayed in a little
shack about twenty miles up the road and said there
would be no problem for me staying there if I mentioned
his name.

I passed mileage signs all the way and it became
a real exciting race as I got closer and closer to the
number that I wanted and it got darker and darker. All
that could be seen was an empty desert with a few
lonely shrubs and, I'm sure, lots of snakes and scorpions. A frightening feeling crept over me and I could
just see my body rotting out in the middle of the desert, probably never found.

After a few more miles I glumly lifted my head -
I was so depressed it had been hanging down around my
stomach - only to see a shack, barely visible but only
a short distance ahead. I almost started dancing on
my bicycle seat, but fortunately I got a grip on myself before I attempted it. It turned out that these
were the people I have been looking for and they said I
could sleep on the dirt floor inside their shack. This
really beat any fancy hotel room. It was just like
heaven for me, or so I thought at first. It was the
greatest relief getting here after having ridden seven-
ty miles - more like 150 considering the strong wind
I was fighting all day.

It didn't take long before I began to think that
I would be safer just to continue riding my bicycle all
night. There were five drunk guys there, all of whom
could have demolished me with one hand and with every
passing minute I became more and more sure that this
was going to be the case. There was one young girl
there about sixteen or seventeen and extremely attractive in a seductive sort of way. She was obviously
living in the shack with the biggest guy of them all.
The second biggest guy was drunk out of his mind and

was doing all he could to hustle her little body. When his attempts were unsuccessful he would give me the most vicious looks and I would just shake in my boots and shyly smile back hoping to give him the impression that I was behind his attempts and encouraging him on. The big guy who lived with the girl did not seem to care one way or the other. One of the guys kept smiling at me and I suspected that he preferred me to his friend's pert little number, though I did all I could to discourage his approaches.

The young girl fed me, and the only thing I could think of was that they were fattening me up for the kill - my last dinner. You can easily see that I was becoming very paranoid, and my imagination was going wild.

CUIDAD OBREGON

The big, mean looking guy who owned the shack and I became pretty good "amigos". This morning we collected firewood then sat around a fire for about an hour. I didn't think I was going to move all day as it was absolutely freezing and sitting around the warm fire made it hard even to imagine riding, let alone getting up and doing it. It finally did start to warm up and I was back on my bicycle again.

The entire day was spent thinking about little things I have done during my lifetime that meant much to me. I am really looking forward to doing them again when I get home; such things as playing golf with Scottie; tennis with Willie and Russ; joking around with Kips; playing hearts & bridge; teaching swimming to little kids again; fish and chips at the White Spot; sitting at the beach with my harmonica; kicking a soccer ball around with Brownie; basketball games Sunday afternoon; working with the teen program; hot showers; Sunday dinners (roast and my favorite potatoes); Sunday night curling; hockey. Some new things I would like to do are to build a cabin, go to art school, work on my book, surf in Hawaii, photography, get a dog, etc.

I did another 85 miles today still against my friend the wind. I got into Cuidad Obregon slightly before dark to be greeted with stares, laughter, shouts and whistles. Although it was getting dark there was no way I could stay in this town.

GUAYMAS

Well, I made it. I've really only got two gears left, and possibly three, that are at all useable. The others have been worn down so that if I do switch into them they only slip.

I was just given a good sniff of good old Guaymas when the wind suddenly changed direction and I had to struggle the rest of the way against a very strong headwind. I was becoming more and more furious though I should have expected it. If that wasn't enough, the back wheel on my bicycle became more and more wobbly as I rode along, and it eventually became so bad that I had to get a lift the last couple of miles into Guaymas.

I've been getting more little hurts lately and I'm becoming a cry-baby, as I was the first week of my trip.

I went to a bicycle shop to get my bicycle wheel straightened as well as other little repairs on things that had gone wrong all at once. I also bought a pair of leather gloves - the most money I've spent for a long time - but very necessary as my hands are freezing when I start out riding in the cold of the early morning.

I phoned my parents to tell them I was planning on doing an extra 500 or 600 miles up to Las Vegas before heading to Los Angeles, then Hawaii.

" ... i used to 'think'
so hard
about how i thought
i should be ...

now i 'am'
so easily
who i can be."

HERMOSILLO

It was very hard to leave this morning as the people were so good to me and the country is just beautiful. I went to the post office again to see if my money had come. I was supposed to have $50 there. I don't know why I even rode in as I was sure that it was not going to be there. I was right.

It was a pleasant riding day for a change as I had the wind slightly at my back for once. This meant that I ride much of the day in high gear - something I have not been able to do for a long time. I only stopped twice the whole day for a total of 15 minutes. Apart from two small road-side cafes, there was no other sign of life all that day.

I found a trailer camp outside the city and decided to pitch my tent there. I was looking for a spot when an older fellow came over and began asking me questions as my bicycle had aroused his curiosity. He invited me to have dinner with him and his wife and also to stay in their trailer out of the cold. They were very thoughtful people. We all went to bed early as they, too, like to see the sun come up in the morning.

MAGDALENA

I have to be the happiest guy in Magdalena right now. I just completed one of my toughest rides and I am especially happy to have it over with and still be alive. I rode a total of 125 dangerous miles and no less than six trucks came within inches of wiping me out. Two of these actually ran me completely off the road and into the bushes.

The first thing I did when I got to Magdalena was to pay a little visit to the Red cross to have my posterior looked after. It has been a definite and constant concern for quite a while and the pain is starting to get unbearable. I saw a Spanish-English doctor, so I was told, but he was as much a Spanish-English doctor as I was an English-Spanish bicycle rider. I told him that my bottom was "mucho malo", which means very sick. I didn't know the word for pain so I could only hope that he understood what I meant. He didn't even look the situation over, but did seem quite sure of my problem. He gave me some medicine for what I am sure was meant for blisters. It is unlikely I would have blisters after four months of riding so I suspect something like boils, but hope that isn't my trouble.

I was really lucky as the doctor said I could spend the night at the Red Cross. It couldn't have come at a better time as I'm extremely low on money as a result of my failure to get money in Guaymas.

NOGALES

Today was a most enjoyable riding day. It was only sixty miles to the border so I took my time so that I could enjoy Mexico to the fullest on the last lap before entering the United States.

All I would like to remember about my last day in Mexico is the ride I had. I would certainly like to forget my last Mexican city which I expect is like all border towns and no indication of what Mexico is really like. I have nothing good to say about the last Mexican town, which is really a poor way to end a tour of a most beautiful country.

I rode past an elementary school and was greeted by derogatory hollers and yells, and the kids did not

hesitate to throw anything that was in their immediate
reach.

Nogales was filled with tourists and tourist
shops run by Mexicans with tourist-trapping intentions.
I talked to quite a few of the tourists, many of which
had only come across the border to buy souvenirs so
that they could say they were in Mexico - enough said!

I ran into two American girls from Chicago and we
went for some tacos on the Mexican side of the border
before heading across to the American side.

When we crossed the border the first thing I did
was to go to a grocery store and buy a loaf of bread
and a jar of peanut butter. The feast took place on
the floor in a coin laundry, where I also got my
clothes washed and phoned my parents to send money by
Western Union.

After the clothes were dry, the girls and I set
out to find a place for me to stay. They were heading
up to Tucson as they had friends there that they could
stay with. Although I was invited along, I refused as
I didn't want another guilty conscience. They gave me
the address, however, and told me that they were sure
I would be welcome there when I arrived tomorrow evening. We tried hotels for me to stay at but they
were much too expensive; we tried the police station,
but they said it was impossible; we tried a trailer
park, but there was absolutely no room.

All our attempts were unsuccessful so the three
of us headed back to the Mexican Nogales. We didn't
search long before we were tempted into a restaurant
by the smell of french fries. It was back to the
American side again after our little meal and we
headed straight for the Western Union office. My
money had arrived and after a few slips and cartwheels,
I had to think again about some place to sleep.

I just can't seem to get myself away from Mexico
as the three of us headed back across the border

again. We found a nice cheap place to stay and it did not take much, at this time, to persuade the girls to stay here also for the night. Although we were all very tired, sleeping was made impossible as our conversation turned to bed bugs and scorpions. We just lay there all night itching and worrying about being attacked. I had the added problem of stomach pains from being constipated, not to forget my sore bum.

TUCSON

In the morning we staggered back across to the American side and after a big breakfast we bade each other a sad good-bye. I've still got bruises on my arm from where they kept nudging me to keep me awake at breakfast.

I was very tired all day but still rode as hard as I ever had as it was great getting back onto a good road again. It was sixty-six miles to Tucson but I was able to cover the distance in just under three and a half hours. The riding conditions were so fantastic that I just smiled and sang as I rode.

My singing is usually unbearable even to me, but today it didn't bother me in the least.

Today my plans underwent another change, but as always these new ones aren't very definite. Instead of spending a month in Hawaii, I am only going to stay there a couple of weeks, so I can get back to riding before I'm too much out of shape. I plan to return to Los Angeles after Hawaii and to head back east, up to Maine, then back across Canada to the West Coast, instead of just riding up the west coast of the States to Vancouver. I may have to take more rides in cars, but hope to do another 7,000 miles on my bicycle. I have to be home at the start of June for my lifeguarding job which is the reason that I will have to cheat on rides. I am really looking forward to seeing Canada, as well as the New England States.

FLORENCE

Unbelievable is the only word to describe today.

I went to the bicycle shop first thing in the morning in the hope that my bicycle had been fixed. I had taken it in last evening and the fellow said it probably wouldn't be ready for a few days. I tried to stress my need for haste to him but there was a line-up of about 25 bicycles ahead of me. He told me, however, to try this morning just in case they were able to get to it. Jim, at the college bicycle shop, had the greatest and most heart-warming surprise for me. The three guys who work there stayed after their regular hours and worked on my bicycle. Besides changing the tires and putting on a new back rim as I had asked, they checked and cleaned the bike thoroughly. Jim told me that I needed a new chain as the other one had stretched, which was, I suppose, the reason it was always slipping. He hadn't put a new chain on as he thought that I might not be able to afford it - he was right. They didn't charge me for their labor but only for the price of the tires and new frame. Pride in their work and pleasure in doing things for people were more important than the money, although it is a necessity to have enough.

On the way out of town, I stopped at a drive-in for a milkshake and met a group of people. A girl in the group invited me to her place to go horseback riding. It was something I really wanted to do but I also wanted to be in Florence before dark. After serious consideration I decided on the latter as I was really in the riding mood. She did, however, go to her house where she got her bicycle and rode with me about five miles out of town.

" ... the more open we are
the less we seem strangers ...
... i've known people i've just met
better than some people
i've known for years ...
... i've known people
who i've become strangers with ...

... i just hope
we're always open ...

... you're too precious to be a stranger."

I am sure glad now that I decided to push on towards Florence instead of spending an extra night in Tucson. If I had remained in Tucson I doubt that I would have met the Clemens, the most beautiful family in the whole world. It must have been fate or something.

The meeting and the development of our close friendship all began just after I had arrived in town. It was fairly dark, and I was exhausted from lack of sleep. I pulled in at a gas station at what I thought was the outskirts of a fairly big town. I could only think about finding a Salvation Army or YMCA to have a shower and to crash there. A guy about fortyish, and decked out in traditional suit and tie came over and asked me where I was from. After he had asked me a bit about my trip, I asked him if he knew of any Salvation Army place or YMCA in town. It was then that he informed me that I was already in the centre of town. I just couldn't believe it. He then asked me if I would join him and his family at his house for dinner and said that I could sleep in the guest house. I was sure that I was hearing things but he assured me that he was serious. I was dirty and grubby, stinky and sweaty, and here he was a good fifteen years older than I, all dressed up and inviting me to his house for dinner and a place to sleep and he had only known me for a matter of minutes. It wasn't long before we were as close as two people could be. Dr. Clemens' openness and honesty paved the way to a communication where we had an amazing understanding of each other in the shortest time. It was as if we had known each other for years rather than only a matter of a few hours. Bill's wife, Beth, and their five kids (Gi-Gi: 12 years old; Bill: 11 years; Mike: 9 years; Tim - alias "Little Brock": 7 years; and Boo-Boo: 5 years), were all as friendly and warm as Bill Sr.

After dinner Bill had to go back to work for awhile so the kids and I tootled on various musical instruments, on all of which they completely showed me up. I decided then to try my luck at their basketball hoop with Bill, Jr., Mike and L.B. (Little Brock), where I again went down to defeat. From there it was to the ping-pong table where I was demolished and embarrassed by Beth. I finally realized I was beaten, so Beth, the kids and I went to a highschool basketball game as I realized at last that spectating was my place. As in most small towns, everybody knows everybody, so I had many stares being a stranger in town. I found out later that many people had mistaken me for Chuck, Bill's brother, who was now married and in Los Angeles.

After everyone else had gone to bed, Bill and I stayed up to all hours talking like two best friends who hadn't seen each other for a long time. They only interruption in the yapping was when we would guzzle down another beer. I think the cans can still be seen today hanging from his chandelier. Mine were the crushed cans, as we were trying to see who was keeping pace. We had completely lost count and will have to wait until the morning when we are better aware of our senses to tally them up and get a winner.

We finally both just passed out after he had promised me that tomorrow would be a very action-packed day. I was sure that I was going to face the new day with a very sore head, but it will have been well worth it.

FLORENCE (second night)

Bill was more than right when he said I would have an action-packed day. I spent the day playing basketball, eating, trying to get Bill's jeep started, trying to ride donkeys that didn't want to be ridden, eating, getting my hair cleaned and styled, getting a new bicycle chain, eating , going to a pro-football game in Phoenix, eating a huge steak dinner, playing ping-pong and wrestling with the toughest and cutest little kids. All these things added up to a most enjoyable and action-packed day. It didn't really matter what I was doing - it was the people I was with that made the day memorable.

I also met some great people who gave me the name of a doctor who runs a chain of health foods and who wants me to meet him tomorrow regarding sponsoring the rest of my trip.

PHOENIX

What can I say! This was one of the saddest moments of my life. We had all become so attached that leaving was like breaking away from the security of understanding people and starting out into a whole new world of strangers. It was a most frightening thought but I knew, and they knew, that I had to hit the road again. I stood there with tears in my eyes and heart for what seemed the longest time.

> " ... *if you won't be honest with me*
> *because you're worried*
> *about hurting me* ...
>
> ... *you'll hurt me so much more*
> *if i find out*
> *you were dishonest.*"

I spent the entire next day down at the health food office trying to work out an agreement, and getting my bicycle and equipment ready for my ride ahead. I plan on trying to get my best distance on my bicycle in one day, so I am starting out from Phoenix tonight at midnight and heading towards Las Vegas, some 300 miles away. If the conditions are right I hope to make it there in 24 continuous hours of riding. The 300 miles is all through the desert so I would like to get this stretch over as quickly as I can.

> " ...when i speak
>   i'm saying
>   what i already know,
>
>   when i listen
>   i want to know
>   more than i'm able to say ...
>
> ...when i argue
>   i need to be right,
>
>   when i discuss
>   i want to share ...
>
> ...i hope my desire to love,
>   is stronger than my need
>   to be right."

LAS VEGAS

The riding today was scary - then frustrating. Just after I started out three drunks pulled up beside me and in the foulest language you could ever imagine, they told me to get off the road or they would find great pleasure in making me obey their commands. Like the chicken I am, I told them that maybe it was a good idea for me to get off the road and so I hid in a little store until they left.

After I had gone a little further about three police cars pulled me off the road, much surprised that a person was riding a bicycle out of town at such a ghastly hour. I was finally able to persuade them that although I was nuts I had no bad intentions, so they let me continue.

When you see the name of the city that I stayed at tonight, please don't think that I was able to make the 300 miles on my bicycle - I didn't. I rode 200 miles in 17 frustrating and exhausting hours before a man found me half dead on the side of the road. I say frustrating and exhausting because I had expected that the distance from Phoenix to Las Vegas would be flat as I had always pictured a desert to be. Also, I was told by a couple of people that this would be as good a place as any to try and go the greatest distance in one day.

It was just a couple of miles out of Kingman when I was completely exhausted. I found myself at the side of the road and with the last bit of strength left I bent my neck over to the side of my prone body to throw up.

I was soon brought to life by the sound of brakes. I opened my eyes to see a car that had gone past me backing up in my direction. The man who picked me up, to whom I will always been indebted, took me into Kingman. He told me that he was going all the way to Las Vegas and that I was welcome to accompany him, but I wanted to ride if I could find enough strength to do so by tomorrow.

My intention to stay in Kingman was soon discarded when we were informed that three bodies had been found that very day, and there was no way that I wanted to be number four. I also talked to the mother of a girl who was one of only two survivors in one of Arizona's worst automobile accidents where seven persons were killed. I accepted the ride to Las Vegas with pleasure.

I tried to locate Mr. and Mrs. Dickey when I got into Vegas but I was unsuccessful. I left word at the hotel desk that I was in town and that I would call again in the morning. I then phoned Mrs. Bernanda French, a friend of the Schussmans'.

She was everything they told me about her - extremely talented and creative.

* * *

When I first got up, I phoned the Dickeys. It was really nice to hear their voices again and they invited me out for dinner that evening and then to hear Liberace who was performing at their hotel. I did my washing before going to the newspaper and radio station for interviews. I am beginning to hate doing this publicity work already as these interviews are very time-consuming - in fact, my entire day was taken up pretty well. This just won't do.

At the radio interview, both Archie Campbell and myself were interviewed at the same time. He is a comedian in the south, famous for his role in the production "Hee-Haw". He invited me to his show for tomorrow night.

That evening I went to Caesar's Palace where I was to meet the Dickeys. I even had a date for the evening which was a real thrill. Well, at least it was a change. The Dickey's along with a business associate of his from Alberta, my date, and myself, all went to see Liberace and Julie Budd. Julie Budd was only 16 and her singing ability and appearance is similar to Barbra Streisand's. The show was excellent and was especially entertaining to me as the piano is my favorite instrument (although I can't play a note myself) and it was played tonight by a real master.

It was 3:30 a.m. before I crawled into Mrs. French's house, but she had left the door unlocked as she had expected that I would be quite late. I have to be up early tomorrow as I have a TV interview first thing in the morning. I am just dreading the thought of waking up early. Sleep is of the utmost importance to me right now.

LAS VEGAS (third night)

I was up at the God-awful hour of 7:30 this morning, for the interview. I looked forward to seeing Archie Campbell that evening and just wandered around having a look at lively old Las Vegas. I had heard a lot about its gambling and night-life, but it was beyond my comprehension. The city was lit up like I could never have imagined. The gambling, to me, was quite depressing as I saw many people who couldn't drag themselves away even though they were having a bad night.

I am going to head for Los Angeles tomorrow so as to be there a few days before my flight to Hawaii. Besides, I have to work something out with the agents of the company that is going to sponsor the remainder of my trip. I am also really looking forward to getting to Palm Desert where the Bremers and McLeans are vacationing. They are both friends of our family.

SEARCHLIGHT

I hit the road really late today. It was about 1:00 before I was finally able to get away as I slept in after my late evening again last night.

Just before leaving town I stopped at a Fried Chicken place and the people there gave me all the pizza and chicken I could eat as well as all I could drink, and they filled a bag full of chicken for the road.

I forgot about the time change today. It was going to get dark an hour earlier than usual as I had crossed a time zone coming into Las Vegas. It was a very dangerous ride today because the roads were narrow and all the losers from gambling in Las Vegas were zooming along about 90 miles an hour. There must have been a lot of losers as I seldom saw a car going the speed limit. What made it more dangerous was that the people from Vegas were undoubtedly under the influence of alcohol.

I was lucky to even see Searchlight when I reached it, it was just a small place with a couple of stores, a motel, a couple of gas stations, and of course, a bar where I am presently situated. It is really freezing and I'm not too optimistic about finding a warm place to stay. I just met an old-timer however, who lives in the hills, and he informed me that there was a run-down shack up near him. He wasn't kidding about it being run-down as the holes were as big as the walls. But it did have an old sofa that made things a little more comfortable, although I'm sure it has seen many rats in its day. I only hope this isn't one of those days. I went to bed early as I want a nice fresh start in the morning.

TWENTY-NINE PALMS

And so ended one of my strangest days.

I was up by 7:30 after very little sleep worrying about whether or not the rats were going to get me. There was an unbelievably strong wind when I woke up and it was really a wonder that the shack was still standing. Fortunately the wind was at my back. If only I had a sheet for a sail I'm sure with this wind that this would have been all the power I needed. I did the first 42 miles in about two hours, but my luck wasn't going to hold out and I was only able to manage 120 miles in the next 12 hours. In all, I did 160 miles in 14 hours.

PALM DESERT

I was really, really weak when I got up this morning and the possibility of making it to Palm Desert, only 60 miles away, looked very doubtful. I was anxious to see the Bremers and McLeans, however, so I pushed on although I took many more rest breaks than usual.

With just 45 miles to go, I phoned my parents to get final instructions on where I was supposed to get my airplane ticket and where I was to meet them.

I did some more thinking about my own future today as I rode along. I have been trying to decide between physical education and social work. As it is right now I am leaning towards physical education teaching. My thoughts then went to how physical education should be taught.

I think that many times the competition in physical education takes away much of the enjoyment of playing different sports. People should learn to enjoy and express with their body, but instead many people dread going to their physical education classes. Some people, on the other hand, enjoy the classes because of the competition. These, I feel, are in the minority. As a result the physical education classes are geared to that minority.

Fortunately, the second half of the day was nothing like the first as far as bicycling goes, I was feeling much stronger and pedalled like crazy towards Palm Desert. I nearly had another accident, however. I was going down an extremely steep incline when I had another flat tire - my seventh, I think - and it was very difficult to control my bicycle at the top speed. I was really proud of myself as I started to fix it myself, something I've never done. However, when my air pump wouldn't work I had to hitch a ride a couple of miles to a gas station where one of the attendants repaired it.

About 12 miles before Palm Desert, I went through Palm Springs and the people were exceptionally friendly which put me in good spirits. The mountains in this area are really beautiful but I was amazed to see the dreadful pollution hovering around the mountains. It came from Los Angeles which is over a hundred miles away. Most of the people around here don't notice it but I could really see and feel the difference today coming in from Twenty-Nine Palms. I guess it was more noticeable to me because I was on a bicycle.

The moment I got to where the Bremers were staying I had my second flat tire of the day, and the eighth of my trip. The Bremers weren't there so I assumed they must have gone out for dinner. The manager and a few of their friends were on the lawn beside the hotel pool and they invited me over for a beer. I then phoned the McLeans who invited me out for dinner. It was great to see them again and they invited me over for a swim at their apartment before I continued on towards Los Angeles. I then went back to the Bremers who, by this time, had returned, and we all went to bed early for the long day of relaxation that was ahead of us tomorrow.

PALM DESERT (second night)

First thing in the morning, I drove Mr. Bremer and a friend of his up to one of the golf courses, then he lent me his car to go to the university.

Before dinner I was a victim of another one of Mr. Bremer's many talents (or so he has been telling me). He skunked me in our first game of crib, let me sneak a win in the second game, then really proved his crib ability in the third game when he walked away with an easy victory. We then had dinner and spent a most enjoyable and relaxing evening watching television. After they went to bed, however, I sneaked out to the kitchen to practice up on my cribbage.

PALM DESERT (third night)

Most of today was spent around the swimming pool. Mr. Bremer and I fixed my flat tire. Actually, Mr. Bremer did most of the work and I was head cheerleader. In the afternoon we went over to visit the McLeans.

LOS ANGELES

After travelling for five months I have been in many cities but there is not one that comes even close in challenging my nomination of Los Angeles as the ugliest city. I can't help it if I sound cynical and even though I was critical of the people there, I was no better myself. Within the course of one day I was in the same rut as they were in many respects. My criticism isn't made with a destructive intent, but only to make people aware of what they're doing to themselves. I feel that they get themselves into a rut and they can't get out mainly because they won't think about it.

LOS ANGELES (second night)

This morning I rode out to U.S.C. which is U.C.L.A.'s big rival in basketball. These universities are rated number one and number two in basketball in the United States and it is particularly interesting because they are both in the same city. They clash in just a few days so it was very interesting for me to go from one to the other and feel the excitement in the air. After that I went to the Museum of Art to have a look around.

I rode about fifty miles in all today around Los Angeles. I should be resting when I stop at a place, but bicycles are just so convenient in the cities.

LOS ANGELES (third night)

I put a lot of miles on my bicycle today just looking around. In the afternoon I went to a park and sat by a creek. I feel very lonely as it really is a beautiful park and I would like someone to share it with. I just wrote, read, and played my harmonica and flute - a very relaxing and enjoyable day.

I was just watching a dog. It is amazing how people give their love to a dog. I am sure the reason is that people aren't worried about its reaction to them. I actually think that dogs have it made and it is because they aren't as intelligent as people that they are probably happier. They, as well as other

"*It is better to be seen for who you are,
and be alone,
Than to be accepted for someone you're not,
and be <u>lonely</u>.*"

—Brock Tully

household pets, get all the love they need, have shelter and food. This is all people really need to be happy.

LOS ANGELES (fourth night)

I am getting really excited about my trip to Hawaii and about seeing my parents again.

LOS ANGELES (fifth night)

The whole day today was spent taking pictures.

I went to bed really excited as tomorrow I would have to get up early so that I could be at the airport in plenty of time.

The agency said there was no more news about a decision on how they were going to use me for advertising but told me they would give me a call in Hawaii. I stressed the importance of them calling as if things didn't look very good then I would probably stay in Hawaii an extra two weeks.

HAWAII

I didn't get any sleep last night as I was just too excited. I rode about fifteen miles in the cold to the airport and almost fell asleep many times.

The flight left pretty well on time. I was becoming extremely hungry and I had only one cent in my pocket. By a real stroke of luck the man next to me offered to buy my lunch. He and his wife lived permanently in Hawaii since he retired and he gave me their phone number and address.

My parents were waiting for me at the airport and we went directly to the apartment which was about forty miles out of Honolulu. They informed me on the way there that my ticket was a return ticket, after I had told them I had thrown it away. My bicycle trip

has obviously not made me smarter as I am still doing
stupid things such as this.

After a huge steak dinner, my parents and I retired early so we could get a nice early start on
the beach tomorrow. I was up early but my curiosity
to see Honolulu and Waikiki became too much for me
and I decided to put off the beach until tomorrow.
I've heard so many varied stories about these places
that I wanted to see them for myself and come to my
own conclusions. I ended up riding my bicycle over
fifty miles today but it will probably be the last time
until I return to the mainland. My purpose for coming
here, besides seeing my parents, is to get some rest
before continuing my trip.

My parents' apartment was situated in the poor
section of Hawaii as far as the locals were concerned.
It was right on the ocean and was one of only three
apartments in the entire area. Our apartment was in
a small cove and the water there was usually rough,
which made things very difficult for people who were
older or for those who were just learning to swim.
Its beautiful situation was enough to attract people
just to sit and watch, and to forego the swimming.
The waves were huge but apparently they can be much
higher in this area. Only one mile down the beach is
where they have the world surfing championships. Up
behind our apartment about a half mile inland and at
the base of a mountain is another apartment with a
36-hole golf course, which we are going to try to
conquer in the next few days.

I was really happy to stay in this area rela-
tively secluded from the tourists of Honolulu and
where there were many true Hawaiians. However, I
really never got to know any of the locals as they
seemed to stay away from the tourists as much as they
could and I was obviously regarded as one.

While I was in Waikiki, I rented a surf-board
for a while as the waves there are good for an
amateur to learn on and I really want to learn.

Well, I only rented the board for an hour and
it took almost that long to paddle out to the waves.
By the time I got there my arms had no more strength
and a second trip seemed very unlikely. I've always
wondered when I've seen surfing on TV why the board
never seems to come down on the surfer's head. It has
always puzzled me. Anyway, I finally saw my wave
which was only a small one. Believe it or not, I
caught it on the first try, but only for five seconds.
As I was returning to the surface for a gasp of air,
my board was returning to the water from somewhere
high up in the sky. We met head on and it won as
could easily be seen by a little bump on the top of
my beanie. But I wasn't discouraged. I tried again,
but this time my ride was more in the vicinity of two
seconds. Although I fell off, my board had a very
good ride all by itself all the way in to shore. A
swimmer brought it back out to me and I told him he
could have a couple of rides. One thing I must point
out here is that I have poor vision and the distance
that I can see is very short and blurry. I was able
to see that fellow I lent my board to had green
shorts on. After about 15 minutes when he hadn't
returned, I went around from surfer to surfer,
squinting to see if they were wearing green shorts,
then asking them if they had borrowed my board.
Finally, after about a 45-minute search, my friend
returned with the board, and I was able to return the
board in the nick of time.

The next day I spent relaxing on the beach with
a little seven year old pal I met who lived in the
same apartment. He was the bravest little character
I've ever seen. He would just stand in front of the
thundering waves daring them to throw him back up on
the beach. The waves accepted his dare, and from out
of the white foam his beaming little face would appear.
All of a sudden his whole body was visible as the
water returned to where it had come from and left it's
little battler laughing mockingly in the sand.

My parents and I went to the Hawaiian Open Golf
Tournament the next day. I even had the pleasure of

walking down the fairway talking to Arnold Palmer -
a real thrill to me as I have much admiration for him
as an athelete. I saw Mr. Stevenson again today. He
was the fellow next to me on the airplane who bought
me lunch. He was a member of the golf course where
the tournament was being played and he invited my
father and me for a game.

I've definitely decided to quit riding for awhile
as I've really got the sorest rear end now. I've found
out that I've got hemorrhoids so I will need an operation some day I suppose. I only hope they don't get
worse before I get back to Vancouver.

> " ... *i'm not afraid*
> *of 'growing old'* ...
>
> ... *i'm excited*
> *about 'growing'*
> *as i get older.*"

The next day I had a newspaper interview and the
girl who did the interview invited me mountain-climbing
the next day with some friends of hers. This would be
another new experience for me and something I've always looked forward to doing although I am petrified
of heights. Five of us went, three guys and two girls,
and you'll never guess who was the biggest chicken.
If you guessed me, you're right and it was a very em-
barrassing predicament. I was in charge of carrying
the sandwiches. When we came to a rock face everyone
made it and I was the last one. I was just shaking
as I really do have a phobia for heights. I needed
both hands to climb the face so I left the sandwiches
at the bottom.

I didn't ride my bicycle at all the last part of
my stay in Hawaii. I was actually about to take it
out for a ride one day, but when I discovered that
both tires had gone flat, my laziness got the better of me and I decided I would get them fixed when
I got back to Los Angeles. Instead I wandered down
to the beach and let the sun soak into my body. My
sponsors still haven't phone me, but I decided that

I'm only going to stay in Hawaii two weeks and continue my trip back east regardless of whether or not
I get the financial assistance.

The worst thing that I saw in Hawaii was the violence and there was plenty of it. The Mafia is very
big in Hawaii and especially near the area where we
were staying. A girl had been killed and buried on a
nearby beach. Apparently she had seen some of the
work done by the Syndicate. Also, a policeman had
just been ambushed after investigating the work of the
Mafia. Things like this apparently happened frequently and the power of the Mafia is supposedly very
great. From talking to highschool teachers in the
area, there is said to be a great number of fights
between boys and girls. One of the teachers had
sailed with three other people across to Hawaii from
Los Angeles. It took about three weeks. That is
something I would really like to do.

In the paper this morning I read about a football player who was in a fight with a local Hawaiian.
The football player won the fight, but not the war as
they say. The next night, nine Hawaiians averaging
245 pounds, and that wasn't a misprint, went to the
athletic dorms and beat up everyone in sight. Incidentally, they didn't find the player that was in the
fight. This kind of violence is very common, from
what I'm told. I was actually even scared to go to
a hamburger stand at night as they were always occupied by what appeared to be young toughs.

I wrote thirty letters to people at home and
elsewhere. I've actually got about five times more
than that to write, to thank people who helped me
along the way. I really feel badly that I haven't
written sooner, but it is very hard to find time to
write when you're on the move every day. Although
I don't write much, the people that I've met are
always in my thoughts and it seems so inadequate to
try to put down in words all that these people did
for me.

LOS ANGELES (first night)

This was the beginning of two and a half terrible days that seemed a lot longer - as if they would never end.

I left Hawaii after a beautifully hot sunny day. It was about 11:00 or 12:00 at night when my plane took off and I arrived in Los Angeles about 7:00 in the morning after getting no sleep whatsoever. I still had my two flat tires on the bicycle but the worst of all was the weather. It was cold and rainy and I just felt like hopping on a plane back to Hawaii. I pushed my bicycle to a gas station and got the tires fixed. I then rode thirty miles to my sponsor's advertising agency in the miserable drizzling rain. They hadn't called me in Hawaii regarding a sponsor and financial arrangements. This really upset me as they knew how important it was to me to know and it would have been so simple for the guy just to pick up his phone and call me. I figured that something must have gone wrong and they couldn't contact me. I was wrong. They just hadn't bothered. They still hadn't any more information but tried to convince me that they were still trying. From what I had seen up to now, I was skeptical.

I spent the rest of the day in one of the rooms of the office phoning around to try to get another sponsor. I had no luck. Business, by the way, is making me sicker and sicker. One of the secretaries actually told me how to talk if I was to have any hope of getting a sponsor. The main thing was to be dishonest and to throw in as many lies as possible to build up your own story. This advice came from a very good person who was only telling me this if I was to hope for any chance of success. It was essential to play it cool and act as if you were doing them a favor. The aim of the whole game was to do everything you could for yourself and you were the winner if you could get more out of the other person. Working together and helping each other was completely out. The idea was to get the other person to come to you. You mustn't be too friendly or the other person would know you were open to be used and would exploit you to the limit. The whole game then was to get out of the other person as much as you could and this was usually measured in terms of money.

However, I still did have a little faith left in people. I finally was able to contact a bicycle company and the fellow there said that he was interested and asked me to come down to his office some five miles away. I rode there in the pouring rain and got completely soaked, but I was too excited about the thought of getting another sponsor that I barely noticed. I really noticed it on the way home, however, as I was now really upset and the little faith I had left was dwindling fast. He had told me to come back tomorrow when another fellow came in. He could have told me this on the phone and saved me a lot of trouble and misery. But it wasn't any skin off his back so I guess it wasn't really important - a very common attitude that I've seen so often.

I then phoned Bob, Sandra, and Ami, the people I stayed with the night before I left for Hawaii, and they told me that I was welcome to come over. I rode about ten miles in the pouring rain and it was extremely dangerous in the traffic as, if you've ever ridden a bicycle in the rain you'd know that the brakes are almost non-functional in wet weather. It really didn't bother me though and I rode along singing and smiling as I had somewhere to go and it is such a good feeling to be heading for a house where there are good people. It was especially good to see them again after all the bad things I went through today.

LOS ANGELES (second night)

I slept in until 2:00 in the afternoon. I just couldn't believe I had slept that long. It must have been a way of escaping from all the misery and anxiety I had yesterday. If it was, I was going to have another long sleep tonight as today was again filled with tension and my near nervous breakdown in Acapulco was coming back to me now in Los Angeles.

I went to see the people at the bicycle place who were interested in sponsoring me. Naturally the fellow wasn't there and the ho-hum attitude of the fellow I was talking to made the chance of any return to their office completely out of the question. I wasn't going to chase them around. They would have to look elsewhere to find someone to play their games.

I then went back to the advertising agent's office, and I wasn't too surprised to find that there was no change. They still had no idea how they were going to use me to advertise their product. Two girls who worked as secretaries in the office offered me a place to stay out by the ocean. I was really in need of the ocean at this point to relax me, so I couldn't think of a better place to go. I was very grateful for the invitation and after putting my bicycle in their car we all headed out to their place. After a lovely dinner we went for a walk on the beach. It was really nice to talk to sensitive people after those I had seen today.

Generally it was a day of running around doing nothing and I was becoming very tense as a result. I'm going to get out of Los Angeles as soon as I can.

POMONA

I stopped at the advertising agency on the way out of town and informed them that this would be the last they would be seeing of me. I told them that I was heading east by way of Phoenix and if they had any further word that they could tell me when I phoned on my arrival there.

My bicycle is in very bad shape right now so I stopped at the first bicycle shop I saw to get it fixed. The guy there was really nice, so I stayed there long enough so that he could fix my bicycle properly.

RIVERSIDE

It was around 11:00 when I got to the University of California in Riverside. It had just started to drizzle, so I decided to stay there until it had passed over. During my wait I met many really good people so I decided to stay here for the night.

As it turned out I was really lucky that I remained in Riverside as there was one of the worst sandstorms in a long time on the desert. These sandstorms come up very suddenly and this one would have caught up with me in the middle of the desert with no protection.

PALM DESERT

It was a fantastic day for riding. There were few cars on the road, no wind, and just a perfect temperature. I stopped in Palm Springs and watching the people, this time both old and young, made me very depressed. I became especially depressed by the young guy who was vegetating on the corner and who was really up on the latest hip jargon. He was so busy worrying about his choice of "cool" words that he really didn't hear what anyone was saying. If he did manage any type of conversation it usually was about the latest drug scene, and who got busted this week.

BLYTHE

It was another beautiful sunny day for riding and I did over a "century" again today. (This is bicycle language for 100 miles.) I am actually quite sore now but it doesn't even compare to that pain I went through the first week after I left Vancouver. I have a lot of little injuries and ailments right now. I've got my painful friends the Hemorrhoids, I've got dandy blisters from my new running shoes, and I've picked up a bit of a cold. I am not looking forward to having a hemorrhoid operation but I suppose I should accept the condition as an occupational hazard of bicycling. To add to my little problems my throat seems to be continually clogged regardless of my cold, my vision is getting progressively worse which is really hard to imagine as it was so bad already, and my teeth need attention, especially one little devil that prevents me from eating on the left side of my mouth. Otherwise I'm in perfect health!

At the moment I am sitting in an A & W in this petite town of Blythe. While I was sitting there I noticed an older couple staring at me from their table. I tried not to take any notice, but shortly afterward they both came over to my table. They had just come from Mexico, and had seen the TV show that I had been on. They had noticed my bicycle and little Canadian flag on my pack and thought that possibly it could have been me that they had seen. It was quite a coincidence but I was glad for it as they were very friendly and enjoyable people. She was Mexican and he was originally from Canada. They were now living in Vancouver which made it even more of a coincidence.

After leaving my thoughts turned to my regular routine, that I always dread, of finding a place to stay. Whenever I'm really in trouble, I usually head for the local police station. They said that it was impossible for me to stay in the jail as it wasn't allowed. They said that I could stay in a nearby park that was regularly patrolled. It was just freezing tonight so I was tempted to rob a bank or something so I could be sure of being thrown in jail and therefore I would have a nice warm, secure place to sleep.

> " ... *it's easy to love those*
> *who are the most loving* ...
>
> ... *but what about those*
> *who need love most?*"

FLORENCE

This is the third consecutive day of beautiful riding. I am growing to like the desert more and more

every day. The mountains are simply fantastic. There
are flat ones, pointed ones, round ones and every
other shape you could think of. I can't believe how
wrong my ideas of the desert had been. I thought all
desert were the same - just miles and miles of sand.
But there is all kinds of growth that doesn't require
water, and it can be just as beautiful as the lush,
green valleys that I saw through Mexico, or the mountains with the creeks running along the roadside bor-
dered by tall trees, or the plains, or the rolling
hills near the Appalachians, and on and on. It is just
wonderful to see the way different growths have adapted
to their land and weather conditions. The openness and
freeness of this area really brings peace to me.

I accomplished a real first today and was terribly
proud of myself. I had my eleventh flat tire in the
middle of the desert and so was nowhere near help. I
therefore was forced to fix my own tire. I changed it
and repaired it all by myself - it sure was an amazing
feat for me.

Unfortunately, though, today wasn't all roses -
in fact the second part of the day was downright
miserable. About 4:30 I heard a little banging noise
from my back wheel after having already covered eighty
easy miles with the wind. Then my wheel started to
wiggle and wobble and soon became impossible for
riding. I therefore had to get a ride all the way to
Phoenix which was all downhill. It was exasperating
to have my bicycle in the back of a pick-up truck and
be looking out the window! Anyway, I was very happy
to get a ride and I was very fortunate that they were
going to Phoenix.

When I got into Phoenix I gave Dr. Bill a phone
call in Florence to tell him of my arrival and that I
would be in Florence by tomorrow. Beth told me he was
in Phoenix on business. She got in touch with him and
he phoned me back at the phone booth in a gas station.
I really needed to see his good, sincere face again as
I am presently feeling very depressed. He told me to
stay where I was and he would try to get out of his

meeting as soon as he could. It was people like the gas station attendant that have gotten me so depressed. He was a big fellow who obviously power-tripped because of pride in his size and I'm sure he would take the smallest excuse to prove his strength. He told me not to hang around the gas station as he didn't really like my looks. I believed him, judging by his instant disapproval of my presence. Anyway, I wasn't going to provide him with that little excuse that he was looking for so I waited beside the road for Bill.

Bill arrived shortly and all my worries and problems were forgotten and we headed out happily to his home some 60 odd miles into good old Florence - the "dreamiest city" of them all. Both times I've seen the Clemens I've been really down, but I couldn't ask for a better cure. They are probably the main reason for my change in plans to go back across the States at such a southerly point.

FLORENCE (second night)

I got up just in time to see the kids coming home for lunch from school. The openness and communication between Bill, Beth, and the kids, continues to amaze me. As far as they are concerned it is such a natural thing for them, but it amazes me as it is such a rare thing when speaking generally of people. The result in this family that is so close and thrives onlove is that they have the warmest and most affectionate kids I've ever seen. The reason, I'm sure, is largely due to the fact that Bill believes in and enjoys his job as a doctor because he wants to help people and is concerned about their happiness. He carries this into his family life as well.

> *"we are only children once ...*
> *... but we can keep the child in us*
> *forever."*

Bill and I stayed up until all hours again,
talking about various things. I am still trying to
do everything I can to convince him of Vancouver's
beauty so that he will come up here this summer for
his vacation.

FLORENCE (third night)

I had no choice but to get up early this morning, as I was suddenly awakened by little feet bouncing around on my bed and on me.

After an unsuccessful session at the health food
place, which I decided would be the last time for me
as I would never be able to trust them anymore, I went
over to see John and Trish at the place where I had
gotten my hair washed. It was really great seeing
them again. First, John and I went for lunch and then
Trish and I went for a walk. Trish was interested in
bicycling and after we had met a few more times I became convinced that she could make a trip of this
nature. I've been pushing my trip too hard up to now
and I decided it would be nice to slow down my pace
and the idea of company sounded very appealing to me
now. She really wanted to get away and she assured
me that she was capable of taking on the challenge and
would return home if her company was any inconvenience.
We decided then that it would be a real experience and
we would give it a try. It was nice to see there was
somebody else as crazy as myself. A few other people
have wanted to ride with me, but they were usually
depressed for one reason or another, and I didn't feel
that the trip had been thought out rationally by them,
and that getting away was all they had in mind.

I then went to Bill's office where he gave me a
complete physical examination. As expected, I did
have hemorrhoids but everything else seems to be okay
and I even have a good, strong heart.

I then experienced one of the most beautiful
things of my whole life. Bill took me to see him

deliver a baby. Actually he had promised me, when
the opportunity arose, that he would take me to see a
birth. When the opportunity did arise I was out.
While he was at the hospital he tried three times to
phone before I had come in from shopping. I rushed
down to the hospital as soon as I could and the nurses
showed me to a room where I had to put on a smock and
mask. Bill was motioning to me excitedly from a distance to hurry. My excitement only made things worse,
but I did make it into the delivery only seconds before
the baby's head entered the world. I looked down at
the floor after the baby was delivered only to see a
couple of bare feet poking out from the two baggy legs
of my pants. I was only able to see this, however,
with one eye as I had put the mask on crooked and one
side had gotten caught on my glasses. My appearance
did provoke a few giggles from the nurses. The delivery of the baby was just a fantastically beautiful
thing to see. I must admit I was becoming a little
squeamish and thought I would save the cleaning lady
extra work if I left before the afterbirth appeared
and then the clean-up.

I went back to the house where I had a swim with
the kids, played some more ping-pong, and then we all
went to the Clemens' favorite restaurant for Spanish
or Mexican food.

FLORENCE (fourth night)

Bill told me this morning about an old man who
had just recently built his own coffin. It was the
custom in his country for people to do this and he
had spent much time and effort fixing it up the way
he wanted it as it meant so much to him. He had even
found a natural cross for it in the mountains. Inside
the coffin he put the things that he wanted to take
with him. Well, the coffin was stolen and at this time
the old man doesn't know about it. The whole thing
has to be about the saddest thing, and I can't imagine
what kind of mind would think of something like this.
I can only hope that the person who took it has an

ounce of feeling left so that his conscience will
get the better of him and that he will return it.

Bill and I spent yet another late night and I'm
sure that Beth must be looking forward to my departure
for the sake of Bill's health and diet, as beer isn't
too good for a nice slim-trim waistline. Bill and I
will certainly go along with that.

FLORENCE (fifth night)

After Beth had given me a tour of the town, which
only took a couple of minutes, I went to Mike's and
"Little Brock's" school. I really enjoyed their classes as they were in the younger grades and instead of
the little kids asking me about my trip they would get
off the subject and tell me all about their grandmothers or just anything that came to mind. This was
perfectly fine with me and I finished the lesson having
learnt a lot about grandmothers.

Afterwards I went to the court house to see if I
might sit in on some good trials. The only trial I
had sat in on was in West Palm Beach in Florida.
Unfortunately, there wasn't anything happening today.

FLORENCE (sixth night)

Bill lent me his car so that Tim (L.B.) and I
could go up to Phoenix to see Trish and get the tandem
bicycle. We ran around most of the day getting things
for her that she would require on the trip, then
"Little Brock" and I returned to Florence after having
agreed to meet Trish first thing tomorrow morning.

Bill and I went to bed early tonight as we knew
that tomorrow was going to be a long and hectic day
and we wanted plenty of rest so we could handle it.

FLORENCE (seventh night)

This time Bill Jr., Mike, L.B. and I headed to Phoenix to get Trish. After bidding Trish's family farewell, those three amazing little devils, Trish and I headed back to Florence.

Bill then took me up to Arizona State Penitentiary which was located in Florence. He used to work there as the doctor and so he was able to take me in as his guest. I found it all very hard to believe as I've only heard about prisons and never really thought about what they would be like. It was just like entering an entirely new world surrounded by four big walls. For anyone who had thoughts of wrong doing, they would be very wise to see inside a prison first and I'm sure it would persuade many first-offenders to lead a more honest life.

At Bill's house we all set up my new tent as a rehearsal for those freezing nights in the desert. I sure didn't want to get out there and then not know how to set it up. Oscar, a friend of Bill's, then fixed the tandem bicycle by transferring things from my other bike that we would need, such as my rack, holder for the water jug, and a generator light that was out of order but which they got working.

Bill then took me down to his office to see if my prostate infection, an additional ailment, was showing any signs of improvement. The infection was cleared up but the hemorrhoids were still painful so he gave me something that he hoped would relieve the pain until I could get home for an operation or something.

After another delicious dinner at the Mexican restaurant I took everyone for a short ride on the new bicycle, then we all went to bed early so that we could get up for a bright and early start.

> *" i think*
> *'being on time'*
> *is being thoughtful*
> *of another 'being's'*
> *time."*

"THE DESERT"

We all got up early and "excitement was in the air"! We were all very nervous and Bill was running around taking pictures.

Then came a very hard thing for me to do. Trish had brought too much in the way of clothes and other things. On a bicycle you can only carry the bare essentials as every pound makes riding much tougher. She realized I was sympathetic to her desire for these things and could understand that it was impossible to take so much. She then picked her things up one at a time to receive either a nod of approval or a shake of my head. More often than not it was the negative gesture and I could see her face becoming sadder and sadder but there was no alternative.

Although it looked very much like a storm was coming up, we both knew that if we were going to get away at all we had to leave today. Besides, it would be good for her to see miserable weather and experience some hard times at the start.

Just after we got out onto the lonely highway, it began to hail but it really wasn't all that miserable. It is much easier to take bad times when you're with someone else; you can just joke and laugh it off. This just makes me think again about Willie's poem - how friendship makes happiness twice as good and misery half as bad. About an hour out on the road Bill rode up alongside us to see that we were making out alright - this was very typical of his thoughtfulness. I will always look forward to seeing him and his family again and they will always be in my thoughts.

We had many short little rests as I was quite
worried that Trish was going to overdo it her first
day. It takes a while to get in shape for a trip
like this as I well remember from my first week. In
fact, I was having a lot of pain in the back of my legs
from trying to get used to a new bicycle. The different shape of the seat was also a discomfort and as
a result I got a rash on the inside of my leg from rubbing on the seat. Our pace was much slower than when
I was riding alone, but in no way do I mean to belittle
Trish. I've never seen anyone who had the guts that
she had; it was only that there was no way a tandem
bicycle can go as fast as a ten-speed bicycle.

At one of our stops a couple from Alberta, Canada,
invited us for lunch. I think they were surprised when
they saw two people on a tandem bicycle in the middle
of the desert. It was also threatening rain and the
black clouds lurked over us waiting until we dared to
step from the safety of the people's trailer. It finally did begin to rain and the biting cold worried
me as Trish wasn't really used to this. She took it
all bravely and we ventured on, hoping that by preten-
ding not to care, the clouds and rain would go elsewhere. This happened and we sighed with relief.

We met another couple who invited us for peach
pies. After we left the warmth of their company it
wasn't long before I was sure that we would never make
it to the safety of a little town. I felt much safer
with the new tent I had bought as it could be completely sealed up. My other one was open at one end
which was just too much temptation to a snake sneaking
some warmth in the cold nights. Besides, I had Trish
to protect me. She thought it was the other way, as I
tried to hide my fear.

We rode and rode as nowhere seemed suitable for
pitching a tent. We really didn't want it to be visible from the road so we kept pedalling in hope that
we'd   find a good spot. We finally did find a
place behind some bushes which was just in the nick of
time before we would be completely in darkness. The

thought of pitching the tent in the dark really did
not do anything to excite me. I unfolded the tent
and began to set it up. My hands were so cold and I
rushed as fast as I could so I could climb into my nice
warm sleeping bag. The pegs kept popping out of the
ground as the sand was so soft, the tent kept tipping
over as there was a very strong wind and that sure did
not make things any warmer. Finally, we were able to
get into the tent and as I was zipping up the final
zipper it decided to get stuck. I became so impatient
that I pulled it too hard and it broke. Trish tried
to fix it without success. We now had an opening for
the snakes to come in and my head was directly in
front of it. I couldn't turn around because the other
end of the tent was lower and I would have gotten up
in the morning without any blood in my lower body.
Needless to say I didn't sleep at all - I must admit
it wasn't because of my fear of snakes but because it
went down about twenty degrees and even with three
layers of clothes on we just shivered and shook all
night. The worry of our tent blowing down and the
howling of coyotes didn't make sleep any easier
either. Naturally I pictured coyotes as the most
vicious animals in the whole world. I heard sounds
outside our tent many times so I kept the knife that
Bill had given me in hand all night. Trish assured
me that the sound was from the wind and I wouldn't
have a chance against the wind with my knife.

TUCSON

It was really a pleasure to wake up, or at least
get out of bed this morning. There wasn't a cloud in
the sky and what wind there was was at our back. It
was rather nippy, however, but it would warm up as
the sun rose higher in the sky. With the wind we made
the 35 miles in excellent time and we were at the university about 1:30. We met some really good people
who offered us a place to stay but we had planned on
going to some friends of Trish's mother.

We then went to a store where Trish bought some
warmer boots, and then we rode another five miles to

her mother's friend. Trish is having quite a bit of trouble with one of her knees. We had a shower and dinner and then I listened to records and wrote a few letters.

It really is nice travelling with someone and sharing the beauties of nature, but we are finding little difficulties and conflicts which is only natural as travelling by this method can be very trying at times.

> " ... when i'm wise
>   i see that, often,
>   my anger isn't with others
>
>   ... it's from my expectations
>   of others,
>   to be otherwise."

EL PASO

We started out early this morning on this most gorgeous day. The first five miles were uphill, and this was bad for Trish with her painful knees. My bum is also in worse shape now. We rode about another five miles to the freeway. We decided that because we had a long way to go to Maine and not that much time to do it, that we were going to have to cheat somewhere. It didn't take long before we decided that here was the place to cheat so as to leave the desert behind us. Conditions would be much less miserable in the eastern part of the United States where the towns are closer together. We thought we would try to get all the way to Dallas by hitch-hiking which was about a thousand miles. After waiting a few hours before a van stopped, we were able to get a ride as far as El Paso, about 350 miles, I think.

Trish and I didn't say much the whole way as we both knew that things were over for us, and the ride gave us a chance to figure this out. Our ideas about certain things are just too different and I'm sure now we are both aware of this. When we arrived at the college in El Paso it was about 9:00 and dark. It was here that I told her that we should end our trip. She agreed. We understood and accepted our differences and remained friends. For the rest of the evening I was feeling really down, lost and empty.

FLORENCE (again!)

Well, I'm back in my favorite "dream city" again after a most strenuous and hectic day. This is the third time I've gone to Florence and each time I was feeling really down. I only hope that I can come out of it this time as before. If anybody can change my mood from depression to happiness it would definitely be the Clemens.

The day began when I called Bill from the university. I had tried without success to sell the tandem bicycle to a bicycle shop, but when I was talking to Bill he offered to buy it as he and his family really wanted it, or so he said. I was just going to have my other bicycle shipped out to El Paso so that I could continue my trip. I had to find some way then, to get Trish back to Phoenix. Bill talked me into flying back to Phoenix with Trish where they would be waiting to pick us up. He told me to leave the tandem bicycle at Tita Cooper's house (friends of the Clemens) for the time being. I was really relieved to have my plans worked out as I was getting very tense inside.

The most fantastic feeling in the world was to see the Clemens' warm and smiling faces at the airport. My worries were soon forgotten and I was back in Florence again which is really beginning to feel like my home town.

FLORENCE (second night)

First thing in the morning I went down to Bill's office. The rash on the inside of my leg from the bicycle seat is still quite tender and I've also got a

sore on my bum right at the base of the spinal cord,
aside from the persistent hemorrhoids. Bill found
this sore to be a pilanidal cyst. This is an infection
caused usually by continuing pressure on this area. It
is a common condition with soldiers in Vietnam who are
continually bouncing around in jeeps. It usually requires surgery and becomes so painful that these soldiers have to be sent home. My only wish is that all
these soldiers get pilanidal cysts, not because I want
them to be in pain, but it may end the war. Bill is
sure that I got mine as a result of changing bicycles.
He doesn't think that I will be able to ride again for
a few days until it has completely cleared up.

It was an unusually early night as we were all
completely exhausted.

FLORENCE (third night)

I am really keen to continue my trip on the other
bicycle, but the cyst is starting to be more trouble-
some. It's Saturday today and Bill insists that I
stay at least for the weekend. If I continue now and
the cyst gets worse in some places where I can't get
help then I really will have worries. While Bill made
his morning rounds at the hospital the other Clemens
and myself played in the pool. I then took the kids
out in Bill's jeep.

We returned to the Clemens and then Bill, his
friend from Tucson, the kids and myself headed out
into the desert to hunt for artifacts. It wasn't long
before we found a great spot and our search was re-
warded with Indian pottery that I was later told was
no less than one thousand years old. We were only
able to find small broken pieces and when we returned to Florence we went to a dentist friend of Bill's
who drilled a hole in one so that I could put it on a
chain for my neck. After dinner we all went to bed
early again. These early nights are definitely doing
Bill's diet a lot of good and latest reports in Florence show that beer sales are considerably lower.

FLORENCE (fourth night)

One of the highlights of the day was when Bill
burnt the coffee cake. He lost another argument with
Beth when he claimed that it wasn't his fault that it
tastes better when it's burnt anyway.

FLORENCE (fifth night)

I was going to continue my trip today as the
longer I prolong my departure the harder it is to
leave, both mentally and physically. However, my cyst
is much worse now. I can't sit on it and even walking
is very painful. I'm going to have to stay here for a
few days at least, and I hope that is all as I've
really got the bug to ride again.

I went to the senior highschool today and talked
to a few of the Grade 12 classes. After answering a
few questions about my trip, we discussed people and
prejudice.

> " ... *since i changed thinking*
> *that i can change others,*
> *i've changed ...*

> *... and since i've changed,*
> *i think my thoughts*
> *have inspired others*
> *to change their thinking.*"

FLORENCE (sixth night)

I am extremely happy this morning as I can see
a definite improvement in the condition of my cyst.

I went to a couple of more senior classes for
discussions. I really enjoy being with these people,
and it seems like I know most of the people in the
town already. I have become close to quite a few of
them now and leaving will be more difficult every day.

In the evening Bill and I went up to the school to go over some films on sex. He was giving a talk tomorrow at the senior highschool.

My happiness with the improvement of my cyst was very short-lived. It has become even more painful now and it is looking more and more like my trip is coming to an end. I can only keep my fingers crossed as continuing really does mean a lot to me. It will be like a job half done, and since this venture is the biggest thing in my entire life, to leave it half done is really going to be a big disappointment. What makes it even worse is that I can only sit and wait to see if I'm going to be able to continue and I really don't have the time to wait much longer.

I am really feeling like I want to be alone right now. With something really important on my mind it is hard to be completely "there" mentally when you're with people.

> " ... *i may not be able*
> *to change the world i see*
> *around me ...*
>
> *but ...*
>
> *i can change the way*
> *i see the world,*
> *within me.*"

FLORENCE (seventh night)

I woke up early this morning and I knew that my trip was over. My cyst is hurting more than ever, and I have only avoided facing the fact that even if it does clear up enough that I can continue riding, it will be only a matter of days before it returns again.

I informed the Clemens of my decision at breakfast and Bill assured me that I was making a wise decision. We arranged for a flight out of Phoenix for tomorrow morning and we all spent the day around the pool. I now began to think positively of my abrupt change in plans by thinking about returning home to my family and friends, and that I would now be able to have two months free to work on my book before I start my life-guarding job in the summer. However, deep down inside, I knew that this turn in events was a real disappointment.

The biggest surprise occurred that evening when some of the people from the highschool had a going-away party for me! I cried inside, the happiest tears, knowing that tomorrow I would be leaving some of the warmest, most beautiful people that I have ever met. These people, all of varying ages, have made me feel so welcome and comfortable in what I will always consider my home away from home. I will always look forward to my return.

VANCOUVER

This was to be the toughest and saddest morning of my whole trip. We arrived at the airport in Phoenix just in time for my flight to Vancouver and as I boarded the plane and looked back at the seven Clemens, all smiling and waving, I knew that this was going to be the last time I would be seeing them for quite a while. And this was the saddest moment of my entire trip.

Within a few hours I was to cover another 1,700 miles and arrive at Vancouver International Airport where I was greeted by my family and friends. It was the greatest to see them all again, but it was still sad to think that my most beautiful trip was ended by the biggest "pain in the ass".

*   *   *